CRIMINAL JUSTICE, LAW ENFORCEMENT AND CORRECTIONS

# CHALLENGES TO THE FEDERAL PRISON SYSTEM AND MITIGATION INITIATIVES

# CRIMINAL JUSTICE, LAW ENFORCEMENT AND CORRECTIONS

Additional books in this series can be found on Nova's website under the Series tab.

Additional e-books in this series can be found on Nova's website under the e-book tab.

CRIMINAL JUSTICE, LAW ENFORCEMENT AND CORRECTIONS

# CHALLENGES TO THE FEDERAL PRISON SYSTEM AND MITIGATION INITIATIVES

BRYAN M. WALKER
EDITOR

nova publishers
*New York*

## NOTICE TO THE READER



**Library of Congress Cataloging-in-Publication Data**

ISBN: 978-1-63484-236-5

*Published by Nova Science Publishers, Inc. † New York*

# CONTENTS

# PREFACE

The federal inmate population has increased more than eight-fold since 1980, and the Department of Justice (DOJ) has identified prison crowding as a critical issue since 2006. DOJ's Bureau of Prisons' (BOP) rising costs and offender recidivism present incarceration challenges to both DOJ and the nation. DOJ has implemented three key initiatives to address the federal incarceration challenges of overcrowding, rising costs, and offender recidivism, which includes the return of offenders to prison after release. This book discusses DOJ's initiatives to address federal incarceration challenges; the extent to which DOJ is measuring its efforts; and the extent to which DOJ is coordinating across its components to implement the Smart on Crime Initiative. Moreover, this book examines the 5-year post-release offending patterns of persons released from state prisons in 2005 by offender characteristics, prior criminal history, and commitment offense. It provides estimates on the number and types of crimes former inmates commit both prior to their imprisonment and after release. The book includes different measures of recidivism, including a new arrest, court adjudication, conviction, and incarceration for either a new sentence or a technical violation. It also documents the extent to which the released prisoners committed crimes in states other than the one that released them.

In: Challenges to the Federal Prison System … ISBN: 978-1-63484-236-5
Editor: Bryan M. Walker 

*Chapter 1*

# FEDERAL PRISON SYSTEM: JUSTICE COULD BETTER MEASURE PROGRESS ADDRESSING INCARCERATION CHALLENGES*

*United States Government Accountability Office*

## WHY GAO DID THIS STUDY

The federal inmate population has increased more than eight-fold since 1980, and DOJ has identified prison crowding as a critical issue since 2006. BOP's rising costs and offender recidivism present incarceration challenges to both DOJ and the nation. For example, BOP's operating costs (obligations) have increased over time, and in fiscal year 2014 amounted to more than $7 billion, or 19 percent of DOJ's total obligations. In recent years, DOJ has implemented targeted initiatives in response, and Senate Report 113-78 included a provision for GAO to review these efforts.

This report discusses (1) DOJ's initiatives to address federal incarceration challenges, (2) the extent to which DOJ is measuring its efforts, and (3) the extent to which DOJ is coordinating across its components to implement the Smart on Crime Initiative. GAO reviewed DOJ documentation, interviewed DOJ officials, and compared DOJ efforts with performance measurement and coordination best practices GAO has previously identified.

---

* This is an edited, reformatted and augmented version of a United States Government Accountability Office publication, No. GAO-15-454, dated June 2015.

## What GAO Recommends

GAO recommends that DOJ explore additional data collection opportunities and modify its Smart on Crime indicators, track and address delays in the sentence commutation process, and modify its current evaluation plan to prioritize evaluations among all 18 of BOP's national reentry programs. DOJ partially concurred with GAO's recommendation that it modify its Smart on Crime indicators and agreed with the other two. GAO continues to believe the Smart on Crime recommendation is valid, as discussed in the report.

## What GAO Found

The Department of Justice (DOJ) has implemented three key initiatives to address the federal incarceration challenges of overcrowding, rising costs, and offender recidivism, which includes the return of offenders to prison after release. The Smart on Crime Initiative involves multiple DOJ components and has five key goals, one of which involves prioritizing the prosecution of the most serious cases. The Clemency Initiative is intended to encourage federal inmates who meet criteria that DOJ established to petition to have their sentences commuted, or reduced, by the President. DOJ is now more focused on prioritizing its review of these petitions, which have increased from about 1,600 in 2011 to about 6,600 in 2014. Finally, DOJ's Bureau of Prisons (BOP) recently established a Reentry Services Division (RSD) to facilitate a more centralized approach to overseeing reentry programs and better assisting offenders in their reentry to society.

DOJ has several early efforts under way to measure the success of these initiatives, but its current approach could be enhanced. In particular:

**Smart on Crime Initiative:** GAO found that DOJ's 16 recently established Smart on Crime indicators were well linked to the effort's overall goals. However, in many cases, the indicators lacked other key elements of successful performance measurement systems GAO has previously identified, such as clarity and context. For example, 7 of the 16 indicators are confusing or do not represent the information the indicator name implies, and 13 of the 16 indicators lack contextual information needed to appropriately interpret their results. DOJ officials said they focused their initial indicators on data already available rather than developing new indicators. Although measuring performance can be a challenge for prosecutorial agencies such as DOJ, research indicates that improved data collection and clearly defined goals and progress measures can help agencies develop effective performance measurement systems. By exploring such options, DOJ would be better positioned to more effectively measure its efforts through the Smart on Crime Initiative.

**Clemency Initiative:** DOJ tracks some statistics related to its Clemency Initiative, such as the number of petitions received and the disposition of each, but it does not track how long, on average, it takes for petitions to clear each step in its review process. Such tracking would help DOJ identify processes that might be contributing to any delays. Without this tracking, DOJ cannot be sure about the extent to which the additional resources it is dedicating to this effort are helping to identify and expedite the review of inmate petitions.

**Reentry programs:** BOP has recently developed a plan to conduct evaluations of some of its reentry programs related to psychology treatment services, but it does not have a plan to prioritize evaluations among all 18 of the programs it lists in its national reentry directory. Modifying its current evaluation plan to consider all of these programs would better position DOJ to know the extent to which its investments in programs intended to reduce recidivism are effective.

DOJ's early efforts to implement the Smart on Crime Initiative are consistent with GAO's key collaboration best practices, such as establishing mutually reinforcing strategies. For example, DOJ directed its law enforcement components and United States Attorneys' Offices to coordinate on establishing prosecution priorities and antiviolence strategies nationwide.

## ABBREVIATIONS

| | |
|---|---|
| ATF | Bureau of Alcohol, Tobacco, Firearms and Explosives |
| BJA | Bureau of Justice Assistance |
| BJS | Bureau of Justice Statistics |
| BOP | Federal Bureau of Prisons |
| CRM | Criminal Division |
| DEA | Drug Enforcement Administration |
| DOJ | Department of Justice |
| EOUSA | Executive Office of the United States Attorneys |
| FBI | Federal Bureau of Investigation |

| | |
|---|---|
| FTE | full-time equivalent |
| OCDETF | Organized Crime Drug Enforcement Task Forces |
| ODAG | Office of the Deputy Attorney General |
| OPA | Office of the Pardon Attorney |
| RAC | Reentry Affairs Coordinator |
| RDAP | Residential Drug Abuse Program |
| RSD | Reentry Services Division |
| SCA | Second Chance Act |
| USMS | United States Marshals Service |
| USSC | United States Sentencing Commission |

* * *

July 19, 2015

Congressional Committees

The number of federal inmates under the Department of Justice's (DOJ) management has presented long-standing incarceration challenges in terms of prison crowding, rising costs, and recidivism—the return of inmates to prison or criminal activity after release. As of February 2015, DOJ's Federal Bureau of Prisons (BOP) was responsible for managing the confinement of about 210,000 inmates in 121 institutions, which is more than eight times larger than the inmate population was in 1980.[1] BOP is not responsible for controlling the flow of inmates into the federal prison system, as convicted offenders are placed directly in BOP's custody and care, but it is responsible for confining these inmates safely and securely. As we reported in September 2012, this responsibility can be challenging with perpetual federal prison overcrowding.[2] In fact, despite a decline of about 8,500 inmates since the end of fiscal year 2013—the first decline in decades—BOP reports that its institutions remain about 30 percent overcrowded, housing considerably more inmates than they were designed to hold. DOJ has identified prison overcrowding as a material weakness in annual reports every year since 2006 and noted its reduction as a high priority in 2013 and 2014. Moreover, DOJ's Inspector General has identified detention and incarceration among DOJ's top 10 management and performance challenges every year since 2004.[3]

Further, BOP's operating costs (obligations) have increased over time,[4] and in fiscal year 2014 BOP accounted for about 19 percent of DOJ's total obligations.[5] In fiscal year 2014, BOP obligated about $7.3 billion (an increase of $2.3 billion from fiscal year 2004), and BOP estimates future obligations of about $7.3 billion and $7.8 billion in fiscal years 2015 and 2016, respectively.[6] To ensure that BOP is effectively controlling its operating costs and reducing expenses where practical, we previously recommended that BOP systematically address the deficiencies that its internal reviewers have repeatedly identified, and BOP is working on corrective actions.[7] The prison system involves costs for both incarceration as well as detention—the housing and related security and transportation of persons from the time they are brought into federal custody until they are acquitted or incarcerated. Operating costs for DOJ's United States Marshals Service (USMS), which is responsible for such detention services, were approximately $1.7 billion in fiscal year 2014, and USMS estimates future obligations of about $1.7 billion and $1.6 billion in fiscal years 2015 and 2016, respectively.[8]

In addition to crowding and rising costs, the rate at which previous offenders return to BOP prisons, or recidivate, compounds the incarceration challenges DOJ and BOP face. In fact, 20 percent of federal offenders released from BOP in fiscal year 2010 returned to BOP facilities within 3 years. The return of offenders to the prison system exacerbates existing crowding concerns and contributes to escalating housing costs. We have previously reported that high rates of recidivism mean more crime, more victims, and more pressure on an already overburdened and overcrowded criminal justice system.[9]

We previously reported that BOP's population size is in large measure driven by factors outside of BOP's control, such as law enforcement policies and sentencing laws.[10] In the last few years, DOJ has implemented targeted initiatives, some of which jointly engage multiple components like the Offices of the United States Attorneys and law enforcement agencies to address the concerns of overcrowding, costs, and recidivism. Senate Report 113-78 included a provision for GAO to conduct a review of these recent efforts, given DOJ's department-wide approach.

This report addresses the following questions:

1) What are DOJ's initiatives to address federal incarceration challenges, such as overcrowding, rising costs, and recidivism?
2) To what extent is DOJ measuring its efforts to address federal incarceration challenges?
3) To what extent is DOJ coordinating across components to implement its Smart on Crime Initiative?

To identify DOJ's initiatives related to federal incarceration challenges, we reviewed DOJ's fiscal year 2014-2018 Strategic Plan and other relevant DOJ documentation. The three initiatives that DOJ is implementing are the Smart on Crime Initiative, the new Clemency Initiative, and BOP's newly established Reentry Services Division (RSD).[11] To address all three of our objectives and better understand these initiatives, we reviewed results from DOJ's comprehensive criminal justice review—a review of the criminal justice system intended to identify reforms that would ensure federal laws are enforced more fairly; department budget justifications for fiscal years 2015 and 2016, and Attorney General memoranda. We also reviewed data and documentation on DOJ standards for clemency and the processes by which DOJ evaluates clemency petitions. We interviewed DOJ officials from the Office of the Deputy Attorney General (ODAG), members of DOJ's criminal justice review working groups, and component officials to further understand the department's Smart on Crime Initiative priorities and determine how the clemency standards and the new criteria are used when reviewing clemency applications.[12]

To determine the extent to which DOJ is measuring its efforts to address incarceration challenges with the Smart on Crime Initiative, we reviewed an internal DOJ document outlining actions to measure the success of the initiative, including key indicators, and interviewed DOJ leaders. We also compared the indicators against three of nine attributes we previously identified for successful performance measures: linkage, clarity, and measurable targets.[13] Additionally, we identified a criterion, based on our prior work, about providing adequate contextual information, and we assessed the indicators against the four criteria.[14] For further information describing our selection of attributes, refer to appendix I.

To determine the extent to which DOJ is measuring its efforts related to the new Clemency Initiative, we reviewed DOJ's publicly available data on the number of petitions for commutation (reduction) of sentence received and their disposition from October 2010 through February 2015, given the new Clemency Initiative began in April 2014. We assessed the reliability of these data by obtaining written responses to related questions about steps taken to ensure data quality from DOJ, and concluded that these data were sufficiently reliable for the purposes of our review. We also interviewed DOJ officials responsible for oversight of the initiative.

To determine the extent to which DOJ is measuring the efforts of BOP's new RSD, we reviewed BOP's *Directory of National Programs* to assess the extent to which BOP specified the studies that provided empirical support and the population studied. We also reviewed BOP population data from 1980 through 2015, and inmate characteristic data from 1997 and 2012 to compare inmate population totals and characteristics from those time periods to the present. We reviewed the methodology used by DOJ's Bureau of Justice Statistics to compile these statistics, and concluded that these data were sufficiently reliable for the purposes of our review. We also assessed the extent to which BOP had a plan for conducting and prioritizing future evaluations, in accordance with criteria from the American Evaluation Association.[15] To determine the extent to which DOJ is coordinating across components to implement its initiatives to address federal incarceration challenges, we reviewed documentation and interviewed DOJ officials to identify the components involved in each initiative. We determined that DOJ's Smart on Crime Initiative was the only one that involved multiple components in various aspects of the initiative, so we focused our assessment on this initiative. We reviewed department-wide and component strategic plans and budget justification documents, where available. We compared DOJ's coordination efforts associated with the Smart on Crime Initiative against three of eight key collaboration practices we have previously identified.[16] We did not include and compare DOJ's actions with the remaining five key practices because DOJ's collaborative efforts are largely internal to DOJ and its components, and its efforts are in the early stages. We also interviewed DOJ officials about oversight and implementation of the Smart on Crime Initiative. For more information on our scope and methodology, refer to appendix I.

We conducted this performance audit from July 2014 to June 2015 in accordance with generally accepted government auditing standards. Those standards require that we plan and perform the audit to obtain sufficient, appropriate evidence to provide a reasonable basis for our findings and conclusions based on our audit objectives. We believe that the evidence obtained provides a reasonable basis for our findings and conclusions based on our audit objectives.

# BACKGROUND

## Description of the Criminal Justice System

Incarceration is one of multiple steps in the criminal justice process and many of DOJ's components have specific roles and responsibilities within and across these steps (see fig. 1).

Source: GAO analysis of DOJ component roles and responsibilities. | GAO-15-454.

[a]An alleged offender can also be placed under arrest after indictment (formal charge issued by a grand jury). After being arrested, a person may be detained (held in federal custody) by the U.S. Marshals Service until future proceedings or incarceration.

Figure 1. Steps in the Federal Criminal Justice System Process.

### *Investigation and Arrest*

DOJ's law enforcement components, including the Bureau of Alcohol, Tobacco, Firearms and Explosives (ATF); Drug Enforcement Administration (DEA); Federal Bureau of Investigation (FBI); and the U.S. Marshals Service (USMS), all share responsibility for investigating crimes, obtaining evidence, arresting offenders, and referring matters for prosecution. To do so, these agencies coordinate and collaborate at the federal, state, and local levels to develop law enforcement priorities, provide training resources, and share information and technology. ATF, DEA, FBI, and USMS are also part of the Organized Crime Drug Enforcement Task Forces (OCDETF), which is a nationwide effort to pursue multijurisdictional investigations of major criminal organizations trafficking drugs and laundering the illegal proceeds.

### *Charging and Litigation*

DOJ's Offices of the United States Attorneys are primarily responsible for federal criminal prosecution, meaning that they decide whether or not to pursue charges against alleged offenders and what charges to seek. To carry out this responsibility, the Offices of the United States Attorneys are to collaborate with federal, state, and local law enforcement partners in 94 judicial districts across the country to set district-specific priorities and thresholds that help them make these decisions.[17]

### *Sentencing*

While judges ultimately determine convicted offenders' sentences, Offices of the United States Attorneys have an opportunity to influence their decisions by providing sentencing recommendations to judges.[18] To do this, prosecutors are to consider the merits of each case, taking into account an individualized assessment of the defendant's conduct and criminal history, the circumstances of the case (including the impact of the crime on victims), and federal resources and priorities.

***Incarceration***

BOP is responsible for this step in the process. To carry out its responsibility for the custody and care of federal offenders, BOP currently houses inmates across six geographic regions in 121 federal institutions.[19] After inmates begin their terms of incarceration, they may file a petition to have their sentences commuted (reduced).[20] DOJ's Office of the Pardon Attorney (OPA) has responsibility for overseeing the petition review process.

***Reentry and Recidivism***

BOP and the Offices of the United States Attorneys both have roles to help ensure that offenders properly transition into society and avoid a return to prison or criminal behavior (recidivism) after they have completed their terms of incarceration. Among other activities, BOP provides reentry services to inmates within federal prisons that include drug treatment programs, education and vocational training, and psychology services. BOP also facilitates the transfer of inmates into residential reentry centers, which provide assistance as inmates transition into communities, to include home detention.[21] In its fiscal year 2016 congressional budget justification, BOP notes that approximately 246 residential reentry centers provide housing for nearly 10,000 offenders prior to release into their communities. Additionally, in recent years, the Offices of the United States Attorneys have prioritized reentry efforts and begun focusing on alternatives to prosecution and incarceration. These, as well as other efforts, are discussed later in the report.

## Activities That Have Affected the Size of the Federal Inmate Population

Over time, the federal government has been involved in activities that have modified federal charging practices and sentencing guidelines, which have resulted in changes to the size of the federal prison population. For example, some efforts have resulted in stricter sentencing for offenders and less discretion for judges, while other, more recent efforts have resulted in greater discretion in the prosecution of offenders and more sentencing flexibility. Appendix II outlines examples of these key activities.

## The Importance of Effective Coordination and Program Assessment

Many of the meaningful results that the federal government seeks to achieve, including criminal justice reform, require coordinated efforts among and within agencies. Federal agencies have used a variety of methods to implement collaborative efforts, which can be useful in policy development and program implementation.[22] In prior work, we have found that collaboration is enhanced when coordinating partners follow certain key practices, which can help clarify efforts and facilitate decision making, such as monitoring, evaluating, and reporting on results.[23] Coordinating agencies, such as the components within DOJ, bring different levels of resources and capacities to collaborative efforts. By assessing relative strengths and limitations, collaborating agencies can better leverage resources and operate more efficiently as they work across agency boundaries. Similarly, we have reported on the importance of performance measurement, which involves the ongoing monitoring and reporting of program accomplishments and provides agency managers with information to gauge progress toward preestablished goals.[24] Additionally, our prior work has discussed the benefits of conducting program evaluations, which are individual systematic studies conducted periodically or on an ad hoc basis to assess how well a program is working.[25] In conjunction, or when resources allow for one but not the other, these approaches can better position agencies, such as DOJ, to gauge their programs' effectiveness and improve their overall management and operations.

# DOJ Implemented Three Key Initiatives to Address Federal Incarceration Challenges

DOJ has implemented three key initiatives to address federal incarceration challenges. Each of these—the Smart on Crime Initiative, the Clemency Initiative, and the newly created BOP Reentry Services Division (RSD)—is focused on better investing staff and budgetary resources to curb federal prison population growth, reduce costs, and stem the return of released offenders back into the federal system.

## DOJ's Smart on Crime Initiative Aims to Comprehensively Reform the Criminal Justice System

Of DOJ's three initiatives to address incarceration challenges, the Smart on Crime Initiative is the most comprehensive—involving multiple components and addressing all steps in the federal criminal justice system. Table 1 illustrates who shares responsibility, the effort's key goals, and its anticipated effect on incarceration challenges.

**Table 1. Elements of the Department of Justice's (DOJ) Smart on Crime Initiative**

| Implementation date and key components involved |
|---|
| • AnnouncedAugust 2013<br>• Offices of the United States Attorneys; Bureau of Alcohol, Tobacco, Firearms and Explosives; Federal Bureau of Prisons; Criminal Division; Drug Enforcement Administration; Federal Bureau of Investigation; Organized Crime Drug EnforcementTask Forces; and the United States Marshals Service |
| Key goals |
| 1. Prioritize prosecutions to focus on the most serious cases<br>2. Reform sentencing to eliminate unfair disparities and reduce overburdened prisons<br>3. Pursue alternative to incarceration for low-level nonviolent crimes<br>4. Improve reentry to curb repeat offenses and re-victimization<br>5. Surge resources to prevent violence and protecting most vulnerable populations |
| Anticipated effect on incarceration challenges |
| • Reduce the federal prison population<br>• Reduce rising costs of operating federal prisons<br>• Improve reentry of federal offenders into society upon release<br>• Reduce return of federal offenders back into prison after release |

Source: GAO analysis of DOJ documentation entitled "Smart on Crime: Reforming the Criminal Justice System for the 21st Century." | GAO-15-454.

The Smart on Crime Initiative has several key features, including the following:

- Directing the Offices of the United States Attorneys to develop or update priorities for their districts and reassess their antiviolence strategies with law enforcement partners (federal, state, and local) to investigate and prosecute the worst offenders. This change in prioritization shifts the emphasis away from prosecuting those associated with lower-level crimes who could then be directed toward alternatives to incarceration or referred for state prosecution, if warranted.

- Directing prosecutors in certain drug cases to (1) decline charging offenders with the quantity of drugs necessary to trigger a mandatory minimum sentence[26] if those offenders are low-level, nonviolent drug offenders and meet certain other criteria,[27] and (2) limit the enhancement of mandatory minimum sentences to those offenders involved in the most severe cases.[28]
- Encouraging BOP to consider recommending sentence reductions or compassionate release under an expanded list of medical criteria for nonviolent offenders who have served portions of their sentences.[29] The Smart on Crime Initiative also encourages prosecutors to participate in inmate reentry programs and to use alternatives to incarceration when appropriate.

Many of the Smart on Crime Initiative's features reflect work performed and policies developed over the past several years. For instance, changes in charging practices stemmed from work that began in 2009 with the convening of DOJ's Sentencing and Corrections Working Group, an effort to assess the administration's agenda and priorities on criminal justice issues. Then, in May 2010, the Attorney General issued a memorandum that formalized prosecutors' use of individual assessments when considering charges, plea agreements, and advocacy at sentencing, and underscored the need for fairness and consistency in the administration of the federal criminal laws among offenders committing similar crimes and having similar culpability. Last, just prior to the launch of the Smart on Crime Initiative, in August 2013, DOJ completed an internal, comprehensive review of all steps in the criminal justice system—including charging, sentencing, incarceration, and reentry—to examine which practices are most successful in deterring crime and protecting the public.

## DOJ's New Clemency Initiative Is an Effort to Expedite the Release of Qualifying Inmates

DOJ's new Clemency Initiative is intended to encourage qualified federal inmates to petition to have their sentences commuted, or reduced, by the President. Commutation of sentence has long been considered to be an extraordinary remedy that is rarely granted. According to DOJ, since December 2013, the President has expressed a desire to review more petitions from potentially qualified inmates, and DOJ has pledged to expedite the review of such petitions in order to provide them to the President for consideration. Appropriate grounds for considering an inmate as qualified for commutation have traditionally been, and will continue to include, disparity or undue severity of sentence and critical illness or old age, among other things. Under the new initiative, DOJ's OPA is prioritizing its review of petitions from inmates who meet all of the following factors: (1) currently serving a federal sentence in prison and, by operation of law, likely would have received a substantially lower sentence if convicted of the same offense(s) today; (2) nonviolent, low-level offenders without significant ties to large-scale criminal organizations, gangs, or cartels; (3) served at least 10 years of their prison sentence; (4) do not have a significant criminal history; (5) demonstrated good conduct in prison; and (6) do not have a history of violence prior to or during their current term of imprisonment.[30] The initiative is primarily designed to encourage nonviolent, low-level offenders to apply for commutation; expedite the review process in order to increase the amount of qualified petitions sent to the President for consideration; and address fairness in sentencing.

Table 2 illustrates the component responsible for the New Clemency Initiative, its key goals, and the anticipated effect on incarceration challenges.

**Table 2. Elements of the Department of Justice's (DOJ) New Clemency Initiative**

| **Implementation date and key components involved** |
|---|
| • Implemented April 2014<br>• Office of the Pardon Attorney |
| **Key goals** |
| 1. Expedite DOJ's review of commutation petitions that may be especially meritoriousto assist the President in exercising his executive clemency power<br>2. Encourage and increase the number of petitions filed for commutation of sentence by low-level, nonviolent offenders |
| **Anticipated effect on incarceration challenges** |
| • Address fairness in sentencing and reduce the federal prison population |

Source: GAO analysis of DOJ documentation. | GAO-15-454.

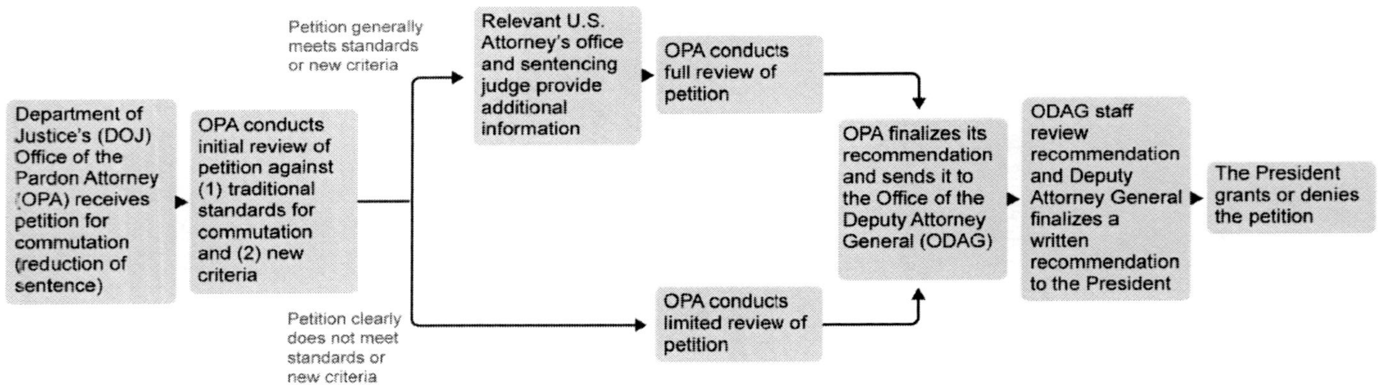


Figure 2. Department of Justice's (DOJ) New Clemency Initiative Review Process.

As part of the Clemency Initiative, the Deputy Attorney General directed BOP to

- notify inmates about the initiative and provide interested inmates with an electronic survey in order to help determine whether inmates meet the criteria under the new initiative,
- inform inmates of the availability of pro bono lawyers and other assistance through the Clemency Project 2014,[31] and
- continue to assist inmates who are applying with the completion of their clemency petitions and submission of the appropriate paperwork to OPA.

Under this initiative, the Deputy Attorney General also directed the Offices of the United States Attorneys to assist in identifying meritorious candidates by offering their views on petitions that appear to meet the criteria after initial screening. Figure 2 highlights the basic steps of the clemency review process.

## BOP Created RSD to Improve Reentry Outcomes and Reduce Recidivism

DOJ approved the consolidation of five branches within BOP into the new RSD in February 2013, and the division was created a year later.[32] BOP's Director reported that the creation of RSD was a critical step in enhancing BOP's focus on reentry. Table 3 illustrates the effort's key goal and its anticipated effect on incarceration challenges.

BOP's reentry strategy has several key features, including the following:

- Promoting continuity and consistency in reentry programs throughout all BOP institutions, which officials believe will improve reentry outcomes. For example, in May 2014, RSD officials prepared the *Directory of Bureau of Prisons' National Programs,* which highlights the standardized programs available to inmates in the areas of inmate treatment and education.[33]
- Further developing specific targets and goals for Reentry Affairs Coordinators (RAC) to help identify available resources to ease inmates' transition to society upon their release.[34] BOP officials told us that each of its institutions now has a RAC in place, and BOP

believes this effort will better prepare inmates for reentry and reduce recidivism, thus reducing prison cost growth.

- Enhancing data collection and analysis efforts to report on recidivism rates. BOP has a bureau-wide committee, chaired by RSD, called the Reentry Oversight Committee. Components of the committee are responsible for overseeing BOP's recidivism data collection efforts. Pursuant to a provision in the Second Chance Act (SCA), BOP is currently collecting criminal history data and plans to report in 2016 on the percentage of released BOP inmates who were arrested (by any law enforcement agency in the United States) or returned to BOP custody within the past 3 years.[35]

**Table 3. Elements of the Department of Justice's (DOJ) Bureau of Prisons' (BOP) Reentry Services Division (RSD)**

| **Implementation date and key components involved** |
|---|
| • Implemented February 2014<br>• BOP |
| **Key goal** |
| • Enable BOP to take a more centralized approach to overseeing reentry initiativesand operations |
| **Anticipated effect on incarceration challenges** |
| • Reduce rising costs of operating federal prisons<br>• Improve reentry of federal offenders into society upon release<br>• Reduce return of federal offenders into prison after release |

Source: GAO analysis of BOP information. | GAO-15-454.

## DOJ's Initial Efforts to Measure Progress Addressing Federal Incarceration Challenges Have Limitations

DOJ has several early efforts under way to measure the success of the Smart on Crime Initiative, the new Clemency Initiative, and BOP's reentry programs, but its current approach has limitations. Specifically, DOJ has created key indicators intended to measure the success of the Smart on Crime Initiative; however, these indicators generally do not show whether or not DOJ is making progress toward the initiative's goals. With respect to the new Clemency Initiative, DOJ tracks data such as the number of petitions received and their ultimate disposition. However, DOJ is not currently tracking how long, on average, steps in the review process take, even though its goal is to expeditiously process petitions for commutation of sentence. Finally, BOP administers nearly 20 reentry programs to reduce recidivism and has begun to consider evaluations in some areas, but it does not have a comprehensive plan in place to prioritize evaluations across its full program catalog to gauge their success.

## DOJ's Recently Developed Performance Metrics for the Smart on Crime Initiative Lack Key Elements of Successful Performance Measurement Systems

In April 2014, DOJ officials developed a plan to assess the implementation of the Smart on Crime Initiative. As part of this plan, DOJ referenced five previously established Smart on Crime Initiative goals and established 16 key quantitative indicators. DOJ reported that these metrics serve as proxies for assessing the effectiveness of the Smart on Crime Initiative's policies intended to achieve these goals. For example, several indicators seek to capture the number of defendants subject to mandatory minimum sentence lengths, while others aim to measure the number of hours spent on reentry or prevention efforts. They also noted that they review these metrics periodically and consider the overall approach to be a first step in what they anticipate will be an iterative design. See appendix III for a listing of these indicators and complete descriptions.

We reviewed DOJ's indicators to determine their effectiveness at measuring progress toward the Smart on Crime Initiative's goals and found them to be lacking across three of four key elements of successful performance measurement systems that we have reported on in the past. These four elements are (1) alignment, or linkage with program goals; (2) clarity; (3) measurable targets; and (4) the inclusion of appropriate contextual information, such as factors inside or outside the agency's control that might affect the measure.[36] Though our prior work includes additional elements, we specifically chose linkage, clarity, and measurable targets because these elements are foundational to establishing successful performance measurement systems regardless of a system's age or relative immaturity. We selected the fourth element, concerning contextual information, because, among other things, many of the indicators associated with the Smart on Crime Initiative are legal and complex in nature.[37]

On the basis of our assessment of DOJ's Smart on Crime indicators against the four elements discussed, we found that all 16 of DOJ's indicators align with (or link to) one or more of the Smart on Crime Initiative's goals, which is a commendable first step in designing an effective performance measurement system.

However, as table 4 shows, we found that 7 of DOJ's 16 indicators are not clear (e.g., are confusing or do not represent what the indicator name implies) and that no indicators have measurable targets. For example, DOJ lists 1 indicator with five additional elements, or subcategories, beneath it, but only two of these five subcategories actually relate to the main indicator above.

We also found that fewer than half—5 of 16—have an established direction (up or down) that indicates progress, and just 3 of 16 provide contextual information, such as factors inside or outside DOJ's control, needed to appropriately interpret the results of the indicators. For instance, DOJ tracks the number of compassionate release decisions granted, but does not explain that the ultimate decision of whether to release an inmate is made by a sentencing judge and is out of DOJ's control.[38] As a result, we determined that the indicators are insufficient to capture progress in achieving DOJ's desired program goals. (For detailed information on how these indicators compare with the four elements we selected, see app. IV.)

**Table 4. Key Findings from GAO's Analysis of the Effectiveness of the Department of Justice's (DOJ) Smart on Crime Key Indicators**

| **Key elements of successful performance measurement systems** | **Summary of findings** |
|---|---|
| **Linkage**<br>Measure is aligned with program goals. | All 16 indicators demonstrate alignment with one or more of the Smart on Crime Initiative's key goals: 7 indicators align with more than one goal, and, taken together, the indicators align significantly more with two of the goals than with the other three. These two goals are:<br>1–prioritize prosecutions to focus on the most serious crimes, and<br>2–reform sentencing to eliminate unfair disparities and reduce overburdened prisons. |

| Key elements of successful performance measurement systems | Summary of findings |
|---|---|
| **Clarity**<br>Measure should be clearly stated and the name and definition should be consistent with the methodology used to calculate it. | Seven of the 16 indicators are confusing or do not represent the informationthe indicator name implies. For example, the names, presentation, and descriptions of 6 of the indicators related to mandatory minimum sentences make it difficult to understand what each indicator is meant to represent individually and how each relates to the others. |
| **Measurable target**<br>Measures should have a numerical goal. Numerical targets or other measurable values facilitate future assessments of whether overall goals and objectives were achieved because comparisons can be easily made between projected performance and actual results. | No indicators have targets, and DOJ has not established which direction indicates success (i.e., whether outcomes of measures should move up or down each year to show progress) for 11 of the 16 indicators. |
| **Provides contextual information**<br>Performance reporting systems should include information to help clarify aspects of performance that are difficult to quantify or to provide explanatory information, such as factors that were within or outside the control of the agency. | Thirteen of the 16 indicators lack contextual information. For example, although clear (named and calculated appropriately), indicators that measure an upward trend in severe offenses (e.g., number of drug defendants with weapon involvement, and number of defendants with an aggravating role adjustment) may be influenced by other factors, such as an increase in prosecutors or prosecutors taking on more cases in general,among other things. Without appropriate context, indicators may be incomplete or misleading. |

Source: GAO analysis of Smart on Crime key indicators. | GAO-15-454.

DOJ believes its key indicators should be thought of differently from traditional performance metrics. The primary reason for this, officials stated, is that the Smart on Crime Initiative is largely aimed at changing prosecutors' behaviors and approaches, and therefore it is difficult to gauge progress quantitatively. Specifically, the Smart on Crime Initiative directs prosecutors to consider individual facts and circumstances of each defendant to a greater extent than in the past when making charging and other key decisions related to each case. As a result, officials said they are hesitant to set targets related to the indicators because targets may create incentives for prosecutors to engage in activities that do not lead to a just and fair outcome. For example, they would not want prosecutors to avoid pressing charges that would appropriately result in a mandatory minimum sentence because of a related target.

Additionally, officials said they are hesitant to establish a direction (up or down) that indicates progress for many indicators because, depending on a variety of factors, progress could be signified by movement in either direction.[39] For example, an increase in the number of mandatory minimum sentences could indicate progress by signaling that prosecutors are prioritizing the most serious cases; however, a decrease in this number could also indicate progress by signaling that prosecutors are applying the Attorney General's 2013 guidance to reserve such charges only for serious, high-level, or violent drug traffickers.

However, the establishment of a direction indicative of success is fundamental to performance measurement systems. Without it, systems cannot reliably assess progress toward goals. Establishing indicators with clear directions may in some cases require identifying links between different indicators that, understood together, indicate progress. Additionally, by failing to set targets, it is possible that prosecutors may not be incentivized to change their practices—some of which the Attorney General has acknowledged have contributed, at times, to unduly harsh sentences. Thus, while DOJ officials are concerned that setting targets may create incentives for prosecutors that lead to unfair outcomes, DOJ may also want to consider the effect of not setting targets—particularly since one of the goals of the Smart on Crime Initiative includes eliminating unfair disparities in sentencing. We agree that it might not be appropriate in every case to create targets early in the development of a performance measurement system, but we underscore the benefits that DOJ could gain by carefully exploring this and other key elements of successful performance measurement systems.

Moreover, officials said that the development of indicators related to the Smart on Crime Initiative is an iterative process and they initially focused on measures and data already available rather than developing new measures that may have required a new data collection effort. This may have also contributed to the challenges they have encountered in creating meaningful performance measures. Nevertheless, DOJ officials said they are constantly exploring how to improve their indicators, including identifying new indicators. For example, in February 2015, the Attorney General issued a memo to United States Attorneys' Offices in which he mentioned five new metrics that drew on United States Sentencing Commission (USSC) data to illustrate the success of the Smart on Crime Initiative.[40] In this same memo, the Attorney General clearly identified directions (up or down) that indicated success. When we asked DOJ officials about these new measures, they confirmed that they are considering incorporating them into their existing set of 16 Smart on Crime indicators.[41]

We acknowledge that measuring progress toward goals within a prosecutorial framework poses challenges in designing measures and collecting data, but research shows that it is possible. For example, in 2004, the American Prosecutors Research Institute published a framework for measuring prosecutors' progress toward achieving widely accepted goals and desired outcomes—such as ensuring safer communities.[42] A follow-up study of the practical application of this framework in two prosecutors' offices provided some empirical support that performance measures may be a valid tool for assessing prosecutor performance relative to goals. However, this follow-up study also found that the prosecutors' offices studied had limited access to data for assessing performance—a challenge DOJ faced as well, according to officials.[43] According to a report published by DOJ's Community Oriented Policing Services, this challenge may be addressed by developing new measures and pursuing additional data collection beyond what is currently available.[44] Last, a 2011 report, published in partnership with DOJ's Bureau of Justice Assistance (BJA), notes the importance of improved data collection and analysis in assessing prosecutor office performance.[45]

DOJ currently relies on data from the USSC to support 10 of its 16 indicators. However, as discussed above, a number of DOJ's indicators lack key elements of successful performance measures. DOJ officials we met with said they are willing to engage in new data collection efforts— apart from what USSC's information system provides—if they determine the benefits outweigh any associated difficulties, such as the costs or staff burdens associated with collecting and reviewing such data independently. By exploring opportunities to collect additional data, DOJ would be better positioned to ensure its indicators effectively measure progress.

Further, a recent report offers examples of what others have done to develop performance measures related to prosecution. Specifically, the Brennan Center for Justice provides examples of how performance measures may be used to track progress toward prosecutorial priorities and goals.[46] For instance, the Brennan Center suggests that Offices of the United States Attorneys could track the percentage of violent crime cases on their dockets, compared with the percentage from the previous year.[47] This approach lines up with the Smart on Crime Initiative's goal of focusing resources on fewer but more significant cases. DOJ officials noted that the success measures suggested by the Brennan Center do not capture the full context and complexity needed to appropriately measure progress. While Brennan's suggested measures may not provide an exact model for DOJ to follow, by considering this framework DOJ may be able to identify the elements it should consider as it continues its efforts to develop more effective performance measures to align with the characteristics of a successful performance management system. For instance, in developing success measures, the Brennan Center (1) defined specific goals for federal prosecution, (2) created related measures for both United States Attorneys' Offices and individual prosecutors, (3) ensured that the measures had clear direction (up or down) that indicates progress toward goals, and (4) provided helpful discussion related to each measure—frequently including prosecutorial incentives that the measures create and in some cases noting how the measures might be refined over time.

DOJ officials have acknowledged the department's currently limited analytical capacity for rigorous assessment of the Smart on Crime Initiative and in the last 2 years, have proposed funding for this function in its annual congressional budget justification. Specifically, in its fiscal year 2015 budget submission, DOJ requested $1.7 million and 8 full-time equivalent (FTE) positions to expand the policy analysis function within the Office of Legal Policy. According to officials, DOJ did not receive a related increase for fiscal year 2015. In its fiscal year 2016 budget submission, DOJ requested $1.5 million and 7 FTE positions for the same purpose. DOJ's budget requests for fiscal years 2015 and 2016 note that this unit could be used, among other things, to assess the Smart on Crime Initiative's effectiveness. Such a unit could help DOJ further refine its measures over time and better isolate the impact of Smart on Crime policies from other influences—such as changes in criminal law or sentencing guidelines.

## New Clemency Initiative Measures Do Not Track Length of Adjudication

As discussed earlier in this report, under the new Clemency Initiative, DOJ officials developed six new criteria to help them prioritize and expedite the review of petitions for sentence commutation (reduction). Although DOJ tracks the number of petitions received, the status of each petition in the review process, and the disposition of each petition, it does not track how long it takes for petitions to clear each step in the review process before DOJ sends the petitions to the White House.[48] As a result, DOJ cannot be sure about the extent to which it is meeting its goal to identify and expedite its review of especially meritorious inmate petitions.

As shown in table 5, the number of petitions for commutation of sentence received during fiscal year 2014 totaled more than the number for the 3 previous fiscal years combined. DOJ attributes this increase in large measure to the launch of the new Clemency Initiative in April of 2014. Further, from fiscal year 2012 through the end of February 2015, the number of decisions (granted, denied, or closed without presidential action) did not keep pace with the number of incoming petitions—and nearly 8,000 petitions were still pending review. Last, DOJ reported that as of December 2014, over 30,000 inmates had requested legal assistance from defense attorneys who are part of the Clemency Project 2014, which was formed to provide pro bono representation to potential applicants under the initiative. As a result, DOJ reported that the numbers of commutation petitions filed by the end of fiscal year 2016 will be significant, and that the cumulative effect of processing these filings will be especially challenging.

Relative to the number of petitions received, it is likely that the number of petitions granted will remain small because commutation of sentence has historically been considered an extraordinary remedy that the President has rarely applied. Nevertheless, to increase its capacity to handle the recent influx of petitions, OPA—which is responsible for reviewing and investigating incoming petitions—received funding for 7 additional positions (for a total of 22) in fiscal year 2015. Additionally, OPA requested 24 additional positions for fiscal year 2016. However, it is not clear if these additional resources will be sufficient to enable OPA to maintain or increase its performance level because DOJ does not track on an aggregate basis how long it takes for petitions to clear each step in its review process.[49]

According to a senior department official, DOJ is not mandated to process petitions within a certain time frame or to analyze data related to the time each step of its review process takes. Rather, DOJ is tasked to process petitions "with all due speed," and therefore best positioned to determine what the appropriate time frames for review of petitions may be.[50] Further, the official explained that all parties involved in DOJ's review chain work diligently to process petitions and generally quickly alert management of any concerns—therefore, from this official's perspective, additional analysis of time frames, step by step, would be redundant. However, DOJ has generally agreed with past recommendations from its Office of the Inspector General (OIG) related to particular aspects of DOJ's clemency petition review process, acknowledging the benefits of analyzing data related to this process that DOJ already has available.[51] Specifically, the OIG reviewed the particular activities of DOJ components working with OPA to review and process clemency petitions and in 2011 made recommendations to improve DOJ components' responsiveness. In 2012, the OIG reported that DOJ components had taken appropriate action to address each of its 10 recommendations.

**Table 5. Number of Petitions for Commutation of Sentence That the Department of Justice Received and Dispositions from Fiscal Year 2011 through May 31, 2015**

| Fiscal year | | | | | |
|---|---|---|---|---|---|
| | **2011** | **2012** | **2013** | **2014** | **2015—partial[a] (10/1/14-5/31/15)** |
| Pending | 3,431 | 1,523 | 2,232 | 2,785 | 7,889 |
| Received | 1,585 | 1,547 | 2,370 | 6,561 | 1,860 |
| Granted | 0 | 1 | 0 | 9 | 33 |
| Denied | 3,104 | 689 | 1,577 | 1,226 | 782 |
| Closed without presidential action | 389 | 148 | 240 | 222 | 651 |

Source: GAO analysis of Office of the Pardon Attorney (OPA) clemency data. | GAO-15-454

Notes: "Received" refers to petitions received during the fiscal year; "pending" refers to petitions at the beginning of the fiscal year for which there has not been closure; "granted" refers to petitions approved by the President during the fiscal year; "denied" refers to petitions rejected by the President during the fiscal year; "closed without presidential action" refers to petitions no longer under consideration because of circumstances such as petition withdrawal, death of the inmate, or inmate release from prison, during the fiscal year.

[a]At the time of our review, data were available only for the first 8 months of fiscal year 2015.

Nevertheless, a gap remains because an overall assessment of how long it takes, on average, for petitions to clear each step in DOJ's clemency review process has not been conducted. The *Standard for Program Management* states that meaningful measures can help program management determine whether or not benefits (outcomes that provide value to intended recipients) are delivered in a timely manner.[52] Tracking the time it takes for petitions to clear each step in the review process, would better position DOJ to determine how well it is meeting the key goal of the new Clemency Initiative—to expeditiously identify and review especially meritorious petitions. Moreover, such tracking would help DOJ address any processes that may be contributing to delays to improve its overall review process.

## BOP's Current Plan for Evaluating Some Reentry Programs Does Not Consider All of Its National Reentry Programs

BOP has developed a national directory of 18 reentry programs, but this directory does not provide sufficient support to demonstrate that its use of these programs is evidence based. To help enhance its knowledge about what works, BOP has recently developed a plan that prioritizes evaluations among some of these reentry programs—those specifically related to psychology services.[53] However, BOP does not have a plan in place to prioritize evaluations among all 18 of its national reentry programs, which would help it ensure the best approach for allocating resources for programs intended to reduce recidivism.

In May 2014, BOP released its first national reentry program directory.[54] According to a DOJ official, ODAG directed BOP to compile this document as a means to (1) review its numerous programs across institutions, and (2) focus on programs with "evidence based" support. According to this official, BOP was to include only those programs that have been rigorously evaluated (or were based on methods that have been rigorously evaluated) and shown to have impact.

In our review of this directory, we found that BOP did not provide sufficient support to demonstrate that the use of its reentry programs is evidence based. Specifically, when assessing the support BOP cites for each program, we observed that

- For 10 of its 18 reentry programs, BOP provided only high-level, general statements about the proven effectiveness of the program or its treatment method(s), instead of providing citations of specific research and discussing how BOP's approach (or approaches) is or is not consistent with this research. For example, for its Parenting Program, BOP states that "research has shown parenting programs for incarcerated parents can improve their self-esteem, parenting attitudes, and institutional adjustment."[55] Similarly, for its Mental Health Step Down Program, BOP states that "the mental health interventions selected for this program have strong empirical support and appear in multiple evidence-based programs registries."[56] As a result, we found it difficult to identify what specific empirical evidence BOP was referring to and the extent to which it may be applicable to the federal prison environment.[57]

- For 5 of its 18 programs, BOP referenced specific studies of state or local reentry programs (or other studies not associated with prison populations) but did not include detailed information about the similarities or differences between the populations studied and the federal prison population, and how the studies might apply to the federal environment.
- For 4 of its 18 programs, BOP cited its own prior evaluations of federal inmates, but these studies assess the impact of programs on offenders released in the 1980s and 1990s, using data from 15 to more than 30 years ago.[58] In recent decades, BOP's inmate population has increased significantly and characteristics of inmates have changed. For example, BOP's population has grown eight times larger than it was in 1980, and has more than doubled since the mid-1990s. Similarly, regarding inmates' characteristics, we previously reported that from 1991 through 1997, the percentage of reported crack cocaine–associated drug offenses increased from 9 percent to 26 percent.[59] Additionally, DOJ's Bureau of Justice Statistics (BJS) reported that from 1997 through 2012, the percentage of inmates 21 years of age through age 30 dropped by 17 percent while the percentage of inmates 41 years of age or older grew by 15 percent.[60] Thus, BOP's reliance on dated evaluations calls into question the extent to which the reentry programs it evaluated in the past continue to be effective amidst changes in inmate population size and inmates' characteristics.

In response to a recommendation we made in July 2013, BOP developed a plan for conducting evaluations among its psychology services programs.[61] This plan addressed 9 programs that are also included among a list of 11 that BOP included in its national reentry program directory under "psychology services."[62] However, BOP's directory also includes 6 programs listed under "industries, education, and vocational training," and 1 program listed under "religious services." Thus, while BOP's plan to conduct program evaluations among its psychology services programs accounts for half of the 18 that BOP lists in its reentry directory, we identified 9 other national reentry programs for which BOP does not have an evaluation plan.

In a written response to our question regarding why it has not created a plan for conducting evaluations among the remaining 9 programs in its national directory, BOP stated that the evaluation of the 9 psychology services programs will take 6 to 10 years, and once those programs have been evaluated, and if sufficient resources exist, BOP will prioritize the evaluation of the remaining 9 programs. Further, in discussing their program evaluation efforts generally, BOP officials cited two challenges. First, rigorous evaluations require substantial investments of budget, time, and staff. Second, it is difficult or impossible to identify appropriate comparison groups for some programs, which are needed for effective evaluation.[63] Additionally, officials believe the three studies they have conducted previously remain valid because the core elements of the programs have not changed. While we agree with BOP officials that evaluations can be time and resource intensive, we have shown earlier that studies conducted more than a decade ago are worth reconsidering in light of changes in the number and characteristics of inmates who participate in such programs today. Further, there are alternative methods for conducting studies absent the ability to randomly assign inmates to reentry programs and comparison groups for evaluation.[64]

The American Evaluation Association (AEA) recommends that each federal agency adopt AEA's proposed framework to guide the development and implementation of its evaluation programs. Among other things, AEA's framework specifies that programs should be evaluated throughout their life cycles for both program improvement and assessment of their effectiveness.[65] By building on its current plan for prioritizing the 9 psychology treatment programs, and prioritizing evaluations among all 18 national reentry programs, BOP could use this framework to consider (1) the applicability to the current federal prison population of reentry program evaluations that others have conducted on non-federal-prison populations, (2) the extent to which there have been significant changes to inmate characteristics since BOP or others conducted previous studies of BOP reentry programs that might affect the effectiveness of current reentry programs, (3) the resource requirements of evaluations that BOP could conduct, and (4) alternative methods for conducting evaluations in the absence of a comparison group or the ability to randomly assign inmates to reentry programs and comparison groups for evaluation. Doing so would better position DOJ to know the extent to which its investments in programs intended to reduce recidivism are effective.

# DOJ HAS COORDINATED EARLY EFFORTS TO IMPLEMENT ITS SMART ON CRIME INITIATIVE

DOJ's early efforts to implement the Smart on Crime Initiative are consistent with GAO's key collaboration practices. In our prior work, we have found that collaboration is enhanced when partners follow certain key practices, such as (1) agreeing on roles and responsibilities, (2) establishing mutually reinforcing or joint strategies, and (3) identifying and addressing needs by leveraging resources—all of which can help clarify efforts and facilitate decision making.[66]

## Agreeing on Roles and Responsibilities

We have recognized in prior work that collaborating agencies should work together to define and agree on their respective roles and responsibilities, including how the collaborative effort will be led, designating a lead body, and establishing oversight for the initiative.

In defining and agreeing on roles and responsibilities, DOJ identified components to address each of its five Smart on Crime Initiative priorities. As table 6 illustrates, DOJ has assigned the Offices of the United States Attorneys a crosscutting role.

**Table 6. The Department of Justice's Smart on Crime Initiative's Goals and Component Responsibilities**

| Smart on Crime Initiative goals | Component responsibilities |
|---|---|
| Prioritize prosecutions to focus on most serious cases | Offices of the United States Attorneys: create district-specific guidelines for federal prosecutions. |
| Reform sentencing to eliminate unfair disparities and reduce overburdened prisons | Offices of the United States Attorneys: adhere to revised department policy regarding charging decisionsto reserve severe penalties for those who have committed more severe crimes.<br>Bureau of Prisons: expand medical criteria that will be considered for inmates seeking compassionate release. |

| Smart on Crime Initiative goals | Component responsibilities |
|---|---|
| Pursue alternatives to incarceration for low-level, nonviolent crimes | Federal law enforcement: encourage alternatives to incarceration.<br>Offices of the United States Attorneys: adopt diversion policies at district level for nonviolent offenses. |
| Improve reentry to curb repeat offenses and revictimization | Offices of the United States Attorneys: designate a prevention and reentry coordinator to focus on prevention/reentry efforts |
| Surge resources for violence prevention and protecting most vulnerable populations | Offices of the United States Attorneys and federal law enforcement: put in place updated antiviolence strategies |

Source: GAO analysis of the Department of Justice Smart on Crime Initiative documentation, *Smart on Crime: Reforming the Criminal Justice System for the 21st Century* (August 2013). | GAO-15-454.

DOJ has delegated the majority of responsibility and oversight of prosecutor efforts and coordination with law enforcement components to implement the Smart on Crime Initiative priorities to the Offices of the United States Attorneys and their individual districts. The Attorney General's call for the creation of district-specific guidelines recognizes that each district's priorities will often depend on local criminal threats and needs, according to DOJ leadership officials. Therefore, the Offices of the United States Attorneys have broad discretion to implement changes in their districts such as updating priorities and thresholds for prosecution, and choosing alternatives to incarceration, such as drug courts and other diversion tactics.

In addition to agreeing on roles and responsibilities, another strong practice is determining who will lead an effort and establishing oversight for implementation. In terms of leadership for the Smart on Crime Initiative, DOJ has determined that these responsibilities rest with the highest offices in the department—the Office of the Attorney General and ODAG. For example, the Deputy Attorney General, through the Attorney General Advisory Committee, holds "call networks" with all of the Offices of the United States Attorneys' districts during which district representatives bring district-level concerns to the committee. These concerns generally involve policy problems that might potentially affect more than one district. Once the concerns are raised to the committee, they are elevated and presented, as appropriate, to the Deputy Attorney General. More complex cases (such as those involving a high-profile defendant, targeting the same individual, nationwide sensitivity, or terrorism) are presented directly to the Attorney General. Through use of this committee and the protocols for elevating any concerns, representatives from ODAG told us they are better able to ensure consistent application of the Smart on Crime Initiative's related guidance and keep track of and address any issues in a real-time manner.

Additionally, in terms of oversight for tracking the Smart on Crime Initiative's outcomes, DOJ created an Initiative Working Group, composed of several components and representatives from the Attorney General's and ODAG's offices. This working group is responsible for activities that include developing indicators to track the success of the initiative, overseeing components' related activities; reviewing progress during quarterly and biannual review meetings; and updating external stakeholders, such as the Office of Management and Budget, on the department's efforts.

## Establishing Mutually Reinforcing or Joint Strategies

We have previously reported that to achieve a common outcome, collaborating agencies need to establish strategies that work in concert with those of their partners or are joint in nature. Such strategies help in aligning the partner agencies' activities, core processes, and resources to accomplish the common outcome.

DOJ has established mutually reinforcing and joint strategies across its components by encouraging and directing their partnerships with one another as appropriate. For example, DOJ's law enforcement components have coordinated with the Offices of the United States Attorneys and other components within DOJ to implement the Violence Reduction Network—a DOJ-wide antiviolence strategy to address law enforcement efforts in high-crime cities across the country.[67] According to DOJ officials, this collaborative effort complements the Smart on Crime Initiative through leveraging resources and reinforcing strategies to federal and local antiviolence strategies consistently. In addition, DOJ has directed many of these same components to coordinate to establish district-level priorities for prosecution and establish and reinforce antiviolence strategies in each individual United States Attorney district.

DOJ has also coordinated with external stakeholders outside of the department on initiative efforts. For example, bolstering reentry programs is a key priority of the Smart on Crime Initiative. The Federal Interagency Reentry Council, established in 2011 by the Attorney General to coordinate reentry efforts and policies across the federal government, continues to help in providing information and materials on reentry efforts related to employment, housing, and other issues under the initiative's reentry-related goals. DOJ has also publically urged the USSC to reduce drug-related mandatory minimum sentencing guidelines for low-level nonviolent drug offenders. The USSC voted in favor of related changes, and on November 1, 2014, the USSC revisions to retroactively reduce sentencing guidelines for some inmates already serving time for drug-related charges took effect. USSC researchers estimate that applying the amendment going forward may reduce the BOP prison population by 6,500 in 5 years and far more over time, while more than 46,000 current prisoners could be eligible to have their sentences reduced by retroactive application of the amendment.

## Identifying and Addressing Needs by Leveraging Resources

Key collaboration practices indicate that collaborating agencies should identify the human, information technology, physical, and financial resources needed to initiate or sustain their collaborative effort to ensure successful implementation of activities. Collaborating agencies bring different levels of resources and capacities to an effort. By assessing their relative strengths and limitations, collaborating agencies can look for opportunities to address resource needs by leveraging one another's resources, thus obtaining additional benefits that would not be available if they were working separately.

DOJ law enforcement components share resources with their state and local law enforcement partners, as well as with the Offices of the United States Attorneys in their districts, to provide and share training, as well as to leverage technology, crime-related data, and intelligence networks. This resource sharing has been enhanced with the implementation of the Violence Reduction Network, as discussed earlier. DOJ has also leveraged resources across several components and entities external to DOJ. For example, DOJ sponsored a June 2014 training focused on federal crime prevention efforts as well as reentry solutions, programs, and resources offered by BOP and individual districts. The purpose of the training was to share information among federal practitioners involved with pretrial and post-conviction decision making and setting district-specific policies and practices related to reentry and prevention. Participants included those from BOP, the Administrative Office of the Courts, federal judges and prosecutors.

DOJ has used its recent annual budget justification to identify the resources it needs across components to sustain the Smart on Crime Initiative.

For example, DOJ requested to reprioritize $173 million in its fiscal year 2015 budget request to support the initiative, directing funding primarily to its reentry and prevention efforts, which is a key priority.[68] Of that amount, the budget request identified $15 million for the Offices of the United States Attorneys to, among other activities, establish Prevention and Reentry Coordinator positions in its judicial districts, engage in other prevention and reentry efforts and provide outreach and training for those districts that develop action plans to prioritize the Smart on Crime Initiative.[69] In that same justification, DOJ requested about $29 million for BOP to continue funding its Residential Drug Abuse Program (RDAP) and reentry programs.[70] In its fiscal year 2016 budget request, DOJ again identified about $15 million for the Offices of the United States Attorneys to expand the prevention and reentry programs associated with the Smart on Crime Initiative and $10 million, including 94 positions, to ensure every district maintains a permanent, full-time equivalent serving in the Prevention and Reentry Coordinator role. For BOP, DOJ requested funding for 150 positions at $146.2 million for the bureau's reentry and recidivism-reducing programs. DOJ also requested funding in both years for an expanded policy analysis function. The 2015 and 2016 budget justifications note that this unit could be used to, among other things, assess the Smart on Crime Initiative's effectiveness.

## CONCLUSION

DOJ's Smart on Crime Initiative, new Clemency Initiative, and BOP's RSD are positive steps in addressing long-standing federal incarceration challenges, and DOJ has taken some initial steps to measure its efforts in these areas. We recognize the challenges in designing any measurement system and the degree to which the complexities of the criminal justice system can make this task even more daunting. However effective measurement is critical to gauging the progress of these initiatives, and DOJ's early measurement efforts have limitations that cannot ensure that DOJ's investments are having their desired effect. In particular, DOJ does not have assurance that its Smart on Crime indicators are effectively measuring progress toward meeting the initiative's key goals because its indicators partially conform to the key elements of successful performance measurement systems. Similarly, DOJ has not adequately assessed the extent to which the new Clemency Initiative is expeditiously identifying and reviewing meritorious petitions because it has not tracked the average time frames for reviewing petitions or identified and addressed any processes that may contribute to unnecessary delays. Finally, DOJ has not fully assessed the effectiveness of its investments in programs designed to reduce recidivism because BOP has not considered all of its 18 national reentry programs in its plan to prioritize future evaluations. Taking action to measure the progress of these three initiatives and the degree to which each is effectively addressing the longstanding challenges of crowding, rising costs, and recidivism would help ensure that DOJ is prudently investing federal resources. Taking these actions now will also allow DOJ to make any necessary changes while each effort is still relatively new.

## RECOMMENDATIONS FOR EXECUTIVE ACTION

To ensure that the Department of Justice effectively measures its efforts to address incarceration challenges, we recommend that the Attorney General take the following three actions:

- explore additional data collection opportunities and modify its Smart on Crime indicators to incorporate key elements of successful performance measurement systems;
- direct the Office of the Pardon Attorney, in conjunction with the Office of the Deputy Attorney General, to (1) track how long it takes, on average, for commutation of sentence petitions to clear each step in the review process under DOJ's control, and (2) identify and address, to the extent possible, any processes that may contribute to unnecessary delays; and
- ensure that the Director of BOP includes, as part of its current evaluation plan, all 18 of BOP's national reentry programs, and prioritizes its evaluations by considering such factors as resources required for conducting evaluations and changing characteristics of inmates over time.

## AGENCY COMMENTS AND OUR EVALUATION

We provided a draft of this report to DOJ for review and comment. DOJ partially concurred with the first recommendation, but agreed with the second and third recommendations. DOJ also provided technical comments, which we incorporated as appropriate.

DOJ partially concurred with our recommendation that DOJ explore additional data collection opportunities and modify its Smart on Crime indicators to incorporate key elements of successful performance measurement systems. Specifically:

- DOJ agreed to continually refine and enhance the indicators to improve their clarity and context, as we recommended. DOJ also noted its reliance on the 16 Smart on Crime indicators in assessing the effect of the overall initiative.
- DOJ did not agree to enact measurable targets for its Smart on Crime indicators. The Department stated that measurable targets for the Smart on Crime Initiative are inappropriate and asserted that prosecutors should make case by case decisions without regard to targets or concern for any other incentive. We agree with the Department's contention that prosecutors should not be forced to choose between charging an individual and failing to advance a measurable target. Independent prosecutorial discretion is a bedrock principle of the nation's criminal justice system and we would not advocate developing and implementing performance measures in a manner that creates perverse incentives for prosecutorial decision-making. At the same time, performance measures and associated measurable targets have been a helpful tool in helping ensure federal programs are making progress toward their stated goals. We recognize that it might not be appropriate to create targets for every indicator early in the development of a performance measurement system. Nevertheless, we maintain that measurable performance targets that are properly developed, communicated, and managed, can aid Department leadership in the admittedly challenging task of assessing progress in the Smart on Crime Initiative.

DOJ concurred with our recommendation that the Department track and address unnecessary delays in the commutation process and reiterated the importance of identifying and addressing unnecessary delays in the clemency review process. Specifically, the Department stated that it would consider our findings and recommendation during the course of its ongoing efficiency reviews.

DOJ concurred with our recommendation that BOP include all 18 of BOP's national reentry programs in its evaluation plan. DOJ stated that BOP will ensure its evaluation plans are inclusive of all national reentry programs, including those that have been previously studied. The Department also noted that it will consider resource constraints as it prioritizes which programs to study in which order. Finally, the Department noted that forthcoming evaluations of programs that had been studied before will consider both changes to program operations and the inmate population.

David C. Maurer
Director,
Homeland Security and Justice

## APPENDIX I: SCOPE AND METHODOLOGY

To identify the Department of Justice's (DOJ) initiatives related to federal incarceration challenges, we first reviewed DOJ's fiscal year 2014-2018 Strategic Plan to determine which components were involved, either directly or indirectly, in the federal criminal justice process. Further, we reviewed DOJ documentation, such as agency memoranda, findings from its review of criminal justice working groups, and component websites to identify three distinct initiatives that DOJ is currently in the process of implementing: (1) the Smart on Crime Initiative, (2) the new Clemency Initiative, and (3) the Federal Bureau of Prison's (BOP) newly established Reentry Services Division (RSD). These initiatives focus on better investing department resources to curb federal prison population growth, reduce costs, and stem recidivism. To better understand all three of the initiatives, we interviewed DOJ leadership, members of DOJ's criminal justice review working groups, and component officials to determine each initiative's intent and purpose, anticipated effect(s) on incarceration challenges, and the departmental resources used to support them, including the funding and number of full-time employees.

With respect to the Smart on Crime Initiative, we also reviewed DOJ's comprehensive criminal justice review results; DOJ's budget justifications for fiscal years 2015 and 2016; and Attorney General memoranda which provided further detail on the initiative's goals. With respect to the new Clemency Initiative, we reviewed documentation related to the standards that DOJ uses when considering clemency for petitioners, the processes by which DOJ evaluates petitions, clemency data, and the application form to determine eligibility requirements. We also interviewed officials from the Office of the Deputy Attorney General (ODAG) to determine how these standards and the new criteria are used when reviewing clemency applications.

To determine the extent to which DOJ is measuring its efforts to address incarceration challenges, we reviewed DOJ and component-specific documents on the Smart on Crime Initiative, the new Clemency Initiative, and BOP's newly established RSD. Specifically, to determine the extent to which DOJ is measuring its efforts related to the Smart on Crime Initiative, we reviewed, among other documents, a key internal DOJ document that outlines the actions the department is taking to measure the success of the initiative, and includes related key indicators, or performance metrics. We also interviewed relevant officials, including from DOJ's leadership offices, to discuss DOJ's plans to measure the effectiveness of the Smart on Crime Initiative.

To determine whether DOJ's 16 Smart on Crime key indicators effectively measured progress, we compared them against selected attributes we previously identified for successful performance measures. In particular, given that the Smart on Crime Initiative and its related indicators are relatively new, we focused on 3 of 9 key attributes of successful performance measures from our previous work that we identified as foundational (linkage, clarity, and measurable targets).[1] We excluded 6 of the 9 attributes because, while important, they are not foundational.[2] For instance, objectivity and reliability (2 of the 6 indicators we excluded) may be difficult to understand without clarity across indicators, and may not be relevant if indicators are not aligned (linked) with program goals. After initially receiving the Smart on Crime key indicators from DOJ, we determined that many of DOJ's indicators were legal and complex—and additional contextual information would be helpful in understanding them. Additionally, we identified instances where contextual information would be necessary to interpret indicator results appropriately. Further, DOJ officials acknowledged the interpretation of the results of many of the indicators depends on other circumstances (context). Therefore, although we were generally satisfied with using the criteria of linkage, clarity, and measurable targets, we also believed it was important to include "provides contextual information," which is 1 of 9 additional key attributes associated with results-oriented management from other previous GAO work.[3] For purposes of this report, we refer to the attributes we use in this report (linkage, clarity, measurable targets, and context) as key elements of successful performance measurement systems. A GAO analyst assessed each indicator against these 4 criteria, another analyst reviewed the reasoning and assessment of the first analyst, and a GAO attorney reviewed and confirmed legal parts of the assessment.

To determine the extent to which DOJ is measuring its efforts related to the new Clemency Initiative, we reviewed DOJ's publicly available information and data. The data we reviewed related to the number of petitions for commutation (reduction) of sentence received and their disposition (pending, granted, denied, or closed without presidential action) from October 2010 through May 2015. We selected this period because the new Clemency Initiative began in April 2014, and we wanted to observe trends before and after it began. We assessed the reliability of these data by obtaining written responses to questions about steps taken to ensure data quality from DOJ, and concluded that these data were sufficiently reliable for the purposes of our review. We also interviewed an official from ODAG with responsibility for overseeing the new Clemency Initiative and obtained written information related to DOJ's process for reviewing petitions for commutation of sentence. We assessed DOJ's process for reviewing these petitions against a criterion from *The Standard for Program Management,* which states that meaningful measures can help program management determine whether or not benefits (outcomes that provide value to intended recipients) are delivered in a timely manner.[4]

To determine the extent to which DOJ is measuring the efforts of BOP's new RSD, we reviewed documents related to the division's creation, its ongoing data and information collection efforts, and other relevant documents. We also interviewed officials from BOP's RSD, as well as its Information, Policy, and Public Affairs Division, who contributed to the thinking and discussions behind RSD's developing reentry strategy before RSD's creation. We reviewed a key document—BOP's *Directory of National Programs*—to assess the extent to which, for each of the 18 reentry programs it listed, BOP (1) included specific studies that provide empirical support, (2) was clear with respect to what population was studied, and (3) provided information about how the population studied relates to federal prisoners. Further, to better understand how past evaluations of reentry programs performed by BOP might be affected by changes over time, we reviewed BOP population data from 1980 through 2015, and inmate characteristic data from 1997 and 2012. Regarding growth in BOP population, we selected the date range of 1980 through 2015 because past evaluations BOP has conducted use data from the 1980s and 1990s, and we wanted to compare inmate population totals from those time periods against totals from the present. We assessed the reliability of these data by obtaining written responses to questions from BOP, and concluded that these data were sufficiently reliable for the purposes of our review. Regarding changes in inmate characteristics, we selected 2012 because this is the year that has the most recent data available, and 1997 because this is the oldest year that data were recorded in a format easily comparable with the 2012 data. We reviewed the methodology used by DOJ's Bureau of Justice Statistics to compile these statistics, and concluded that these data were sufficiently reliable for the purposes of our review. We also assessed the extent to which BOP had a plan for prioritizing and conducting future evaluations, in accordance with criteria from The American Evaluation Association (AEA), which recommends that each federal agency adopt AEA's recommended framework to guide the development and implementation of its evaluation programs. Among other things, AEA's framework specifies that programs should be evaluated throughout their life cycles for both program improvement and assessment of their effectiveness.[5]

To determine the extent to which DOJ is coordinating across components to implement its initiatives to address federal incarceration challenges, we reviewed documentation and interviewed DOJ officials to identify the components that were involved in each of the initiatives. On the basis of our analysis, we determined that DOJ's Smart on Crime Initiative was the only one that involved multiple components in various aspects of the initiative, so we focused our assessment on this initiative. To identify the steps DOJ has taken to coordinate the Smart on Crime Initiative, we reviewed department-wide and component strategic plans and budget justification documents, where available. We then compared DOJ's early efforts to coordinate activities associated with the Smart on Crime Initiative against three of eight key collaboration practices we have previously identified.[6] These three criteria were agreeing on roles and responsibilities, establishing mutually reinforcing or joint strategies, and identifying and addressing needs by leveraging resources. We did not include the remaining five key practices for two reasons.[7] First, DOJ's collaborative efforts are internal to DOJ and its components. Our past work on key collaborative efforts has typically focused on interagency collaborative efforts among multiple departments and agencies. Second, DOJ's internal initiative is in its early stages, and we have generally discussed the remaining key collaboration practices for those interagency collaboration efforts that have been under way for some time. To add additional context to our work, we reviewed DOJ's Smart on Crime Initiative documentation—*Smart on Crime: Reforming the Criminal Justice System for the 21st Century* and its *Smart on Crime Framework* document, which details the activities and oversight of component deliverables and tasks, periodic meetings on progress, work on developing indicators to track the Smart on Crime Initiative's efforts and successes, and other aspects of the department's implementation of the initiative. We also reviewed available Attorney General memoranda that set forth policy changes for the Offices of the United States Attorneys on charging practices; specific tasks and time frames for district-level implementation of the Smart on Crime Initiative's actions, such as setting district-level charging guidelines; and district-level antiviolence strategy work with law enforcement partners. These activities are directly related to the priorities and goals set forth in the Smart on Crime Initiative. Finally, we interviewed officials from several DOJ components to discuss how they coordinated across component agencies to work on activities related to the Smart on Crime Initiative. We also interviewed officials from ODAG and the Office of the Attorney General to discuss oversight responsibilities and district-specific activities to implement the Smart on Crime Initiative's priorities.

# APPENDIX II: EXAMPLES OF KEY ACTIVITIES THAT AFFECTED FEDERAL CHARGING AND SENTENCING PRACTICES

Over time, the federal government has been involved in activities that have modified federal charging practices and sentencing guidelines, which have resulted in changes to the size of the federal prison population. For example, some efforts have resulted in stricter sentencing for offenders and less discretion for judges, while other, more recent efforts have resulted in greater discretion in the prosecution of offenders and more sentencing flexibility. See table 7 for additional examples of key activities that have affected charging and sentencing.

**Table 7. Examples of Key Activities That Have Affected Federal Charging and Sentencing Practices since 1984**

| Key activity | Description | Effect on sentencing or charging of offenders |
|---|---|---|
| Sentencing Reform Act of 1984[a] | Modified sentencing for offenses committed on or after November 1, 1987. | Abolished parole for federal offenders sentenced after its effective date.[c] |

**Table 7. (Continued)**

| Key activity | Description | Effect on sentencing or charging of offenders |
|---|---|---|
| | Established the independent United States Sentencing Commission (USSC) within the judicial branch and charged it with, among other things, developing federal sentencing guidelines[b] | Specified sentencing guideline ranges in terms of time (in months) that offenders should serve given the nature of their offense and other factors. Permitted sentences to depart upward or downward from guideline ranges because of aggravating or mitigating circumstances. |
| Attorney General memorandum (2003) | Established the Department of Justice's (DOJ) policy for federal prosecutors to charge and pursue the most serious, readily provable offense and yield the most substantial sentence. | Resulted in stricter charging of offenders. |
| Supreme Court decision *United States v. Booker,* 543 U.S. 220 (2005) | Found the *Sentencing Guidelines,* which had previously been binding for federal judges to follow in sentencing criminal defendants, to be advisory in nature.[d] | Provided federal judges discretion to sentence offenders outside of the *Sentencing Guidelines.* |
| Attorney General memorandum (2010) | Underscored the need for consistency in sentencing among offenders committing the same crimes. Stated that in order to initiate charges against a defendant, prosecutors must (1) determine that the person's conduct constitutes a federal offense and admissible evidence is sufficient to obtain and sustain a conviction and (2) that the prosecution serves a substantial federal interest, | Reinforced principle that persons who commit similar crimes and have similar culpability should, to the extent possible, be treated similarly and equal justice depends on individualized justice. Accordingly, federal prosecutors when making decisions regarding charging,plea agreements, and advocacy at sentencing must make decisions based on the merits of each case, taking into account an individualized assessment of the defendant's conduct and criminal history and the circumstances relating to the commission of the offense, among other things. |

| Key activity | Description | Effect on sentencing or charging of offenders |
|---|---|---|
| | the person is not subject to effective prosecution elsewhere, and there is no adequate noncriminal alternative to prosecution. Requested federal prosecutors to (1) conduct individualized assessments of offenders' conduct and criminal history, (2) decline to charge the quantity necessary to trigger a mandatory minimum sentence if the defendant meets certain criteria, and (3) ensure that plea agreements reflect the totality of defendants' conduct. | |
| Supreme Court decision *Alleyne v. United States,* 133 S. Ct. 2151 (2013) | Held that any fact that increases the statutory mandatory minimum sentence is an element of the crime that must be submitted to the jury and found beyond a reasonable doubt. | For a defendant to be subject to a mandatory minimum,requires prosecutors to include in the charging document those elements of the crime that trigger the statutory minimum penalty, thereby heightening the rolea prosecutor plays in determining whether a defendant is subject to a mandatory minimum sentence. |
| Attorney General memorandum (2013) | Refined DOJ's charging policy in light of the Supreme Court decision in *Alleyne v. United States*and requested districts to develop prosecutorial priorities. Requested federal prosecutors to consider particular factors when developing district-level investigative and prosecution priorities, including whether (1) the offense falls under explicit DOJ or government-wide priorities, (2) the federal government had primary or | Reinforces an individualized assessment of the extent to which particular charges fit the specific circumstances of the case, are consistent with the purpose of the federal criminal code, and maximize the impact of federal resources on crime. |

**Table 7. (Continued)**

| Key activity | Description | Effect on sentencing or charging of offenders |
|---|---|---|
| | exclusive jurisdiction in the location where the offense took place, and (3) there are effective alternatives to incarceration available to the defendant. | |
| Changes in sentencing guidelines affecting prison term lengths | Sentencing guidelines changed to reduce prison sentence length for future federal drug offenders, and retroactively to incarcerated drug offenders. | Expected to reduce the federal prison population and BOP's operating costs over time, as we reported in September 2014.[e] |

Source: GAO analysis of DOJ documentation and legal rules and decisions affecting sentencing and charging practices. | GAO-15-454.

[a]Pub. L. No. 98-473, 98 Stat. 1987.

[b]USSC establishes sentencing policies and practices for the federal criminal justice system that are intended to provide certainty and fairness in meeting the purposes of sentencing, avoiding unwarranted sentencing disparities among defendants with similar criminal records who have been found guilty of similar criminal conduct while maintaining sufficient flexibility to permit individualized sentences when warranted. 28 U.S.C. § 991(b)(1)(B).

[c]Subsequent legislation established mandatory minimum sentences for many federal offenses.

[d]Judges were still required to properly calculate and consider the *Sentencing Guidelines* and other sentencing goals.

[e]GAO, *Bureau of Prisons: Information on Efforts and Potential Options to Save Costs,* GAO-14-821 (Washington, D.C.: Sept. 30, 2014).

# APPENDIX III: DOJ'S SMART ON CRIME KEY INDICATORS

The Department of Justice (DOJ) created 16 key quantitative indicators that, it reports, act as proxies in assessing the effectiveness of Smart on Crime policies intended to achieve these goals.

**Table 8. Department of Justice's (DOJ) 16 Smart on Crime Key Indicators and Descriptions**

| DOJ key indicator[a] | Description[b] |
|---|---|
| 1. Number of defendants subject to (sentenced to) mandatory minimum sentence under 21 U.S.C. § 841[c] | Defendant was sentenced to a 5-year or 10-year or higher mandatory minimum. |
| 2. (Number of defendants sentenced to) no mandatory minimum | Defendant was not sentenced to a drug mandatory minimum sentence either because the offense did not trigger a drug mandatory minimum sentence or because the provisions of 18 U.S.C. § 3553(f) also known as the "safety valve," applied.[d] |
| 3. (Number of defendants sentenced to) 5-year mandatory minimum | Defendant was sentenced to a 5-year mandatory minimum. |
| 4. (Number of defendants sentenced to) 10-year mandatory minimum | Defendant was sentenced to a 10-year or higher mandatory minimum. |
| 5. No mandatory minimum plus safety valve (number of drug defendants not charged with an offense carrying a drug mandatory minimum that also qualified for the safety valve) | Cases where a drug mandatory minimum sentence did not apply and the safety valve applied. |
| 6. Mandatory minimum plus safety valve (number of drug defendants charged with an offense carrying a drug mandatory minimum that also qualified for the safety valve) | Cases where a drug mandatory minimum sentence applied but the court sentenced the offender without regard to any applicable mandatory minimum sentence in accordance with the safety valve. |
| 7. Number of drug defendants with weapon involvement | Number of drug defendants who received either a guideline enhancement for weapon involvement or a conviction under 18 U.S.C. § 924(c).[e] |
| 8. Number of drug defendants with an aggravating role adjustment[f] | Number of drug defendants who received an aggravating role adjustment under USSG§ 3B1.1.[f] |
| 9. Number of drug defendants with a mitigating role adjustment | Number of drug defendants who received a mitigating role adjustment under USSG § 3B1.2. |
| 10. Number of 851-enhanced charges (number of 851-enhanced mandatory minimum sentences)[g] | Number of drug defendants that received mandatory minimum sentence enhancements under 21 U.S.C. § 851.[g] |

**Table 8. (Continued)**

| DOJ key indicator[a] | Description[b] |
|---|---|
| 11. Hours spent on reentry effortsh–FTE[i] | Number of hours, expressed as full-time equivalent (FTE) positions, spent on reentry efforts by the Offices of the United States Attorneys. |
| 12. Hours spent on prevention efforts–FTE | Number of hours, expressed as FTE positions, spent on prevention efforts by Offices of the United States Attorneys.[j] |
| 13. Number of compassionate release decisions (granted)[k] | Number of compassionate release requests granted. |
| 14. Number of reentry courts[l] | Number of reentry courts Offices of the United States Attorneys participate in. |
| 15. Number of drug diversion courts[m] | Number of drug diversion or specialty courts Offices of the United States Attorneys participate in. |
| 16. Number of commutations[n]–granted | Number of commutation (reduction) of sentences granted. |

Source: GAO analysis of DOJ's Smart on Crime key indicators. | GAO-15-454

Notes: According to DOJ, indicators 2-6 are subsets of the universe composed of the total number of drug defendants who were sentenced under the *U.S. Sentencing Guidelines* (USSG) sections: 2D1.1 (Drug Trafficking), 2D1.2 (Protected Locations), 2D1.5 (Continuing Criminal Enterprise), 2D1.6 (Use of Communication Facility), 2D1.8 (Rent/Manage Drug Establishment), and 2D2.1 (Simple Possession).

[a]Parentheses in indicator names added by GAO for clarity. [b]Descriptions provided by DOJ, with edits added by GAO for clarity.

[c]Under 21 U.S.C. § 841, it is unlawful for anyone to knowingly or intentionally manufacture, distribute, or dispense, or possess with intent to manufacture, distribute, or dispense, a controlled substance, or create, distribute, or dispense, or possess with intent to distribute or dispense, a counterfeit substance, except as authorized by law.

[d]18 USC § 3553(f). The safety valve allows for certain defendants sentenced for certain drug offenses who meet specified criteria not to be subject to mandatory minimum penalties. For the safety valve exception, the court is to consider at sentencing (1) the defendant's criminal history; (2) whether the defendant used violence or credible threats of violence or possessed a firearm or other dangerous weapon in connection with the offense; (3) whether the offense resulted in death or serious bodily injury to any person; (4) whether the defendant was an organizer, leader, manager, or supervisor of others in the offense or was engaged in a continuing criminal enterprise; and (5) the defendant has truthfully provided to the

government all information and evidence the defendant has concerning the offense or offenses that were part of the same course of conduct or of a common scheme or plan.

[e]Generally, 18 U.S.C. § 924(c) prohibits the using, carrying, brandishing, or discharging of a firearm during a drug or violent crime.

[f]Judges are required to consult the *U.S. Sentencing Guidelines Manual* when determining an appropriate sentence and may apply adjustments to a sentence based on aggravating or mitigating circumstances.

[g]By filing one or more notices of prior felony drug conviction under 21 U.S.C. § 851, prosecutors can potentially enlarge a mandatory minimum sentence from 5 to 10 years or 10 to 20 years or life.

[h]For purposes of this indicator, reentry efforts are defined as "all work associated with performing the Offices of the United States Attorneys' duties attendant to a reentry program, including attendance at reentry court meetings or hearings as part of intensive supervision of offenders on supervised release, meetings with incarcerated offenders as part of a program to discuss reentry issues, or other meetings with members of the public or government and non-government organizations to discuss offender reentry issues. In addition, any time spent on training, preparation, and consultation in connection with reentry programs is included."

[i]DOJ officials stated that they use 2,080 hours to calculate one FTE.

[j]For purposes of this indicator, prevention efforts are defined as "all work associated with the Offices of the United States Attorneys' outreach activities designed to prevent crime, particularly violent crime. This includes presentations at government and non-government facilities, and time spent preparing for and arranging such presentations and events." DOJ also confirmed that prevention efforts include efforts related to diversion activities.

[k]Upon motion of the Director of BOP, the court may reduce a term of imprisonment after considering certain factors, if it finds that either (1) extraordinary and compelling reasons warrant such a reduction, or (2) the inmate is at least 70 years of age, has served at least 30 years in prison for the offense or offenses for which the inmate is imprisoned, and a determination has been made by the Director of BOP that the inmate is not a danger to the safety of any person or the community, and that such a reduction is consistent with applicable policy statements issued by the United States Sentencing Commission (USSC). 18 U.S.C. § 4205(g), 18 U.S.C. § 3582(c)(1)(A).

[l]Federal reentry courts manage the reintegration of offenders from prison to the community. Such programs allow the court to impose graduated sanctions and positive reinforcements in a team approach that typically involves a judge, probation officer, assistant U.S. Attorney, assistant federal defender, and contract services provider.

[m]Drug court or specialty court (e.g., alien smuggling courts, veterans courts) programs seek to creatively meet public safety imperatives while avoiding incarceration for

certain offenders. Each of these programs explicitly incorporates some form of judicial involvement in the offender's supervision; thus, courts are primary actors in these programs, and courts must participate in their creation. The goal of supervision in these programs is to identify and address the root causes that led or contributed to the defendant's criminal activity, in the hope of avoiding recidivism. Some of these programs result in a full dismissal of charges, while others result in a probationary sentence or a sentence of little or no incarceration.

[n]Per Article II, Section 2 of the United States Constitution, the President may commute, or reduce, federal inmates' sentences. Commutation of sentence has long been considered to be an extraordinary remedy that is rarely granted. Appropriate grounds for considering commutation have traditionally been disparity or undue severity of sentence, critical illness or old age, and meritorious service rendered to the government by the petitioner, among other things.

# APPENDIX IV: GAO ASSESSMENT OF THE DEPARTMENT OF JUSTICE'S SMART ON CRIME INITIATIVE'S KEY INDICATORS

### Table 9. GAO Assessment of Whether the Department of Justice's (DOJ) Smart on Crime Initiative's Key Indicators Possess Certain Key Elements of Successful Performance Measurement Systems

| DOJ key indicator[a] | Linkage (aligns with one or more program goals) | Clarity | Measurable target/established direction indicative of success[b] | Provides contextual information needed tointerpret the results |
|---|---|---|---|---|
| Number of defendants subject to (sentenced to) mandatory minimum sentence under 21 U.S.C. § 841[c] | Yes | No | No/no | No |
| (Number of defendants sentenced to) no mandatory minimum | Yes | No | No/no | No |
| (Number of defendants sentenced to) 5-year mandatory minimum | Yes | No | No/no | No |

| DOJ key indicatora | Linkage (aligns with one or more program goals) | Clarity | Measurable target/established direction indicative of successb | Provides contextual information needed tointerpret the results |
|---|---|---|---|---|
| (Number of defendants sentenced to) 10-year mandatory minimum | Yes | No | No/no | No |
| No mandatory minimum plus safety valve[d](number of drug defendants not charged with an offense carrying a drug mandatory minimum that also qualified for the safety valve) | Yes | No | No/no | No |
| Mandatory minimum plus safety valve (number of drug defendants charged with an offense carrying a drug mandatory minimum that also qualified for the safety valve) | Yes | No | No/no | No |
| Number of drug defendants with weapon involvement | Yes | Yes | No/no | No[e] |
| Number of drug defendants with an aggravating role adjustment | Yes | Yes | No/no | No[e] |
| Number of drug defendants with a mitigating role adjustment | Yes | Yes | No/no | No[e] |
| Number of 851-enhanced chargesf (number of 851-enhanced mandatory minimum sentences) | Yes | Yes | No/no | No |
| Hours spent on reentry efforts | Yes | Yes | No/yes | Yes |

**Table 9. (Continued)**

| DOJ key indicator[a] | Linkage (aligns with one or more program goals) | Clarity | Measurable target/established direction indicative of success[b] | Provides contextual information needed tointerpret the results |
|---|---|---|---|---|
| Hours spent on prevention efforts | Yes | Nog | No/yes | Yes |
| Number of compassionate release decisions (granted) | Yes | Yes | No/yes | No[e] |
| Number of reentry courts | Yes | Yes | No/yes | No[e] |
| Number of drug diversion courts | Yes | Yes | No/yes | No[e] |
| Number of commutations–granted | Yes | Yes | No/no | Yes |
| Total that met the criteria | 16 of 16 | 9 of 16 | 0 of 16/ 5 of 16 | 3 of 16 |

Source: GAO analysis of DOJ key indicators. | GAO-15-454

[a]Parentheses in indicator names added by GAO for clarity.

[b]"Established direction indicative of success" refers to whether or not an indicator has a defined direction (up or down) that would signify progress; this key element is a subcriterion of "measurable target," which refers to an indicator having a numerical goal.

[c]Under 21 U.S.C. § 841, it is unlawful for anyone to knowingly or intentionally manufacture, distribute, or dispense, or possess with intent to manufacture, distribute, or dispense, a controlled substance; or create, distribute, or dispense, or possess with intent to distribute or dispense, a counterfeit substance, except as authorized by law.

[d]18 USC § 3553(f), also known as the safety valve, allows for certain defendants sentenced for certain drug offenses who meet specified criteria not to be subject to mandatory minimum penalties.

[e]In some cases, we found that indicators were clearly stated and their names and definitions were consistent with the methodology used to calculate them (clarity); however, the indicators lacked information about what factors might influence their results (context).

[f]By filing one or more notices of prior felony drug conviction under 21 U.S.C. § 851, prosecutors can enlarge a mandatory minimum sentence from 5 to 10 years or 10 to 20 years or life.

[g]In one instance, an indicator included contextual information related to its broader interpretation and meaning (context), but the name of the indicator was not consistent with the definition and methodology used to calculate it (clarity).

## End Notes

[1] BOP also confines inmates in secure privately managed or community-based facilities and local jails.

[2] GAO, *Bureau of Prisons: Growing Inmate Crowding Negatively Affects Inmates, Staff, and Infrastructure,* GAO-12-743 (Washington, D.C.: Sept. 12, 2012). In particular, we found that crowding has negatively affected inmates housed in BOP institutions, institutional staff, and the infrastructure of BOP facilities, and has contributed to inmate misconduct, which affects staff and inmate security and safety.

[3] Office of the Inspector General, Department of Justice: *Top Management and Performance Challenges Facing the Department of Justice, 2014,* http://www.justice.gov/oig/challenges/2014.htm.

[4] BOP officials said that any cost savings from the recent prison population decline (and potential future declines) would be relatively small because BOP prisons are still overcrowded by about 30 percent. As a result of this overcrowding, BOP is not in a position to close any facilities in the foreseeable future, and it needs to increase staffing levels to make prisons safer.

[5] This percentage is derived from DOJ's fiscal year 2014 agency financial report. DOJ, *FY 2014 Agency Financial Report* (November 2014). As listed in that report, total obligations for BOP reflect obligations for (1) salaries and expenses, (2) buildings and facilities, and (3) the Federal Prison Commissary Fund, which is a self-sustaining trust that allows inmates to purchase additional products and services above the necessities provided by appropriated federal funds. Since DOJ's annual financial report includes the Commissary Fund in BOP's total obligations, we include it here as well, even though it is not a direct appropriation.

[6] Actual and future estimated obligations are from the President's budgets for fiscal years 2006 and 2016. They include the same categories of obligations for BOP as those included in DOJ's annual financial report, cited above.

[7] GAO, *Bureau of Prisons: Information on Efforts and Potential Options to Save Costs,* GAO-14-821, (Washington, D.C.: September 2014).

[8] These actual and estimated obligations, from the President's fiscal year 2016 budget, include costs for federal prisoner detention as well as related security and transportation.

[9] GAO, *Inmate Reentry Programs: Enhanced Information Sharing Could Further Strengthen Coordination and Grant Management,* GAO-13-93 (Washington, D.C.: Dec. 14, 2012).

[10] GAO-14-821.

[11] There are two forms of executive clemency: (1) pardon, which is granted after release from prison and restores certain rights lost as a result of the pardoned offense (such as the right to vote or sit on a jury), and (2) commutation of sentence, which reduces a sentence—either totally or partially—that is then being served.

[12] ODAG is responsible for advising and assisting the Attorney General in formulating and implementing department policies and programs and in providing overall supervision and direction to all of DOJ's components. The new criteria are six factors that DOJ will now use to prioritize clemency applications from inmates who meet all of the factors.

[13] We excluded six of the nine attributes because, while important, they are not foundational. These six attributes are objectivity, reliability, core program activities, limited overlap, balance, and government-wide priorities. Appendix 1 provides more information about our attribute selection.

[14] Our prior work establishes nine key attributes of successful performance measures. GAO, *Tax Administration: IRS Needs to Further Refine Its Tax Filing Season Performance Measures*, GAO-03-143 (Washington, D.C.: November 2002). Our prior work also establishes nine key attributes associated with results-oriented management. GAO, *Information Sharing: DHS Could Better Define How It Plans to Meet Its State and Local Mission and Improve Performance Accountability*, GAO-11-223 (Washington, D.C.: December 2010). For purposes of this report, we refer to these attributes as "key elements of successful performance measurement systems."

[15] American Evaluation Association, *An Evaluation Roadmap for a More Effective Government,* (revised October 2013).

[16] GAO, *Results-Oriented Government: Practices That Can Help Enhance and Sustain Collaboration among Federal Agencies*, GAO-06-15 (Washington, D.C.: Oct. 21, 2005); *Managing for Results: Key Considerations for Implementing Interagency Collaborative Mechanisms,* GAO-12-1022 (Washington, D.C.: Sept. 27, 2012); and *Managing for Results: Implementation Approaches Used to Enhance Collaboration in Interagency Groups*, GAO-14-220 (Washington, D.C: Feb. 14, 2014.)

[17] DOJ officials explained that a threshold is a limit that must be exceeded in order to pursue a case. For example, a district may decline to pursue financial fraud cases that do not exceed $50,000, unless there are other compelling reasons to do so.

[18] DOJ officials said that judges also receive recommendations from probation officers and defense attorneys.

[19] In addition to these federal institutions, BOP also houses inmates in privately managed facilities and home detention. According to BOP officials, privately managed contract facilities are low security and primarily house non-U.S. citizens convicted of crimes while in this country legally or illegally. Home detention describes all circumstances under which an inmate is serving a portion of his or her sentence while residing in his or her home.

[20] Commutation of sentence is one of two forms of executive clemency (the other form is pardon). Commutation of sentence may reduce a sentence—either totally or partially— that is then being served. Pardon restores certain rights lost as a result of the pardoned offense, and may be granted only after release from prison.

[21] Residential reentry centers provide employment counseling and job placement assistance, financial management assistance, and substance abuse treatment or counseling as well as other services, which may vary by facility.

[22] For the purpose of this report we use the term "collaboration" broadly to include interagency activities that others have variously defined as "cooperation," "coordination," "integration," or "networking." We have done so since there are no commonly accepted definitions for these terms and we are unable to make definitive distinctions among these different types of interagency activities.

[23] GAO, *Results-Oriented Government: Practices That Can Help Enhance and Sustain Collaboration among Federal Agencies*, GAO-06-15 (Washington, D.C.: Oct. 21, 2005), and *Managing for Results: Key Considerations for Implementing Interagency Collaborative Mechanisms*, GAO-12-1022 (Washington, D.C.: Sept. 27, 2012).

[24] GAO, *Managing for Results: Enhancing Agency Use of Performance Information for Management Decision Making.* GAO-05-927 (Washington, D.C.: September 2005).

[25] GAO, *Program Evaluation: Strategies to Facilitate Agencies' Use of Evaluation in Program Management and Policy Making*. GAO-13-570 (Washington, D.C.: June 2013).

[26] Federal statutes set certain mandatory minimum sentences, such as five, ten, or twenty years, that must be served in accordance with law if certain factors such as drug quantity are charged and proven.

[27] According to memoranda issued by the Attorney General, the other criteria the defendant must meet are the defendant's relevant conduct does not involve the use of violence, the credible threat of violence, the possession of a weapon, the trafficking of drugs to or with minors, or the death or serious bodily injury of any person; the defendant is not an organizer, leader, manager, or supervisor of others within a criminal organization; the defendant does not have significant ties to large-scale drug-trafficking organizations, gangs, or cartels; and the defendant does not have a significant criminal history.

[28] When a defendant is involved in certain conduct, such as violence, or has significant ties to large-scale drug-trafficking organizations, gangs, or cartels, among others (21 U.S.C. § 851), prosecutors can file one or more notices of prior felony drug conviction, potentially enlarging a mandatory minimum sentence from 5 to 10 years or 10 to 20 years or life.

[29] Upon motion of the Director of BOP, the court may reduce a term of imprisonment after considering certain factors, if it finds that either (1) extraordinary and compelling reasons warrant such a reduction, or (2) the inmate is at least 70 years of age, has served at least 30 years in prison for the offense or offenses for which the inmate is imprisoned, and a determination has been made by the Director of BOP that the inmate is not a danger to the safety of any person or the community; and that such a reduction is consistent with applicable policy statements issued by United States Sentencing Commission. 18 U.S.C. § 4205(g), 18 U.S.C. § 3582(c)(1)(A).

[30] According to DOJ officials, apart from the addition of these new factors, the clemency review process has not changed.

[31] The Clemency Project 2014 is an external organization independent of DOJ that consists of the American Bar Association, the National Association of Criminal Defense Lawyers, the Federal Defenders, the American Civil Liberties Union, and Families Against Mandatory Minimums, as well as federal public defenders. It was organized in response to the Deputy Attorney General's January 30, 2014, speech to the New York State Bar Association in which he called for assistance in identifying appropriate clemency petitions under this initiative. Its goal is to assist inmates with completing their clemency applications as well as provide pro bono, or free, legal representation.

[32] These five branches were previously part of the Correctional Programs Division: National Reentry Affairs, Chaplaincy Services, Residential Reentry Management, Female Offenders, and Psychology Services.

[33] This directory does not represent all programs offered by BOP institutions. All federal institutions also offer vocational training (such as registered apprenticeships and trades) which are compiled annually in the *Inmate Occupational Training Directory*. Institutions also offer locally developed programs, such as religious services, recreation, education, and reintegration for inmates.

[34] Reentry Affairs Coordinators are primarily responsible for the evaluation, monitoring, and coordination of skill development and reentry initiatives, as well as volunteer program activities in BOP institutions.

[35] See 42 U.S.C. § 17541(d)(3). Under the SCA, at the end of each fiscal year, the BOP Director is required to submit a report to the House and Senate Committees on the Judiciary containing statistics demonstrating the relative reduction in recidivism for inmates released

by BOP within that fiscal year and the 2 prior fiscal years, comparing inmates who participated in major inmate programs (including residential drug treatment, vocational training, and prison industries) with inmates who did not participate in such programs.

[36] GAO, *Tax Administration: IRS Needs to Further Refine Its Tax Filing Season Performance Measures*, GAO-03-143 (Washington, D. C.: Nov. 22, 2002). In that report, we developed nine key attributes of successful performance measures based on previously established GAO criteria, consideration of key legislation, and review of performance management literature. We selected three of these nine criteria for our assessment of DOJ's Smart on Crime Initiative's measures: linkage, clarity, and measurable targets. In another report, GAO, *Information Sharing: DHS Could Better Define How It Plans to Meet Its State and Local Mission and Improve Performance Accountability*, GAO-11-223 (Washington, D.C.: Dec. 16, 2010), we discussed a separate set of nine key attributes associated with results-oriented management based on a previous body of work on this topic. Of these nine attributes, we selected one that addressed the importance of performance measures providing contextual information. For purposes of our current assessment of DOJ's Smart on Crime Initiative's indicators, or performance metrics, we refer to linkage, clarity, measurable targets, and the contextual information as "key elements of successful performance measurement systems."

[37] For more information about why we excluded certain key elements, see app. I.

[38] For more information on this and other indicators, see app. II.

[39] According to DOJ officials, some of these factors include, for instance, changes in criminal law and sentencing guidelines, changes in immigration policies, and changes in the number of federal prosecutors.

[40] The USSC is an independent agency in the judicial branch of government. It was created by the Sentencing Reform Act provisions of the Comprehensive Crime Control Act of 1984, Pub. L. No. 98-473, 98 Stat. 1976. The sentencing guidelines established by the commission are designed to incorporate the purposes of sentencing (i.e., just punishment, deterrence, incapacitation, and rehabilitation).

[41] We did not evaluate the five new metrics against elements of successful performance measurement systems because they are not yet part of DOJ's official Smart on Crime indicators.

[42] American Prosecutors Research Institute (APRI), *Prosecution in the 21st Century: Goals, Objectives, and Performance Measures*, (February 2004). APRI no longer exists, but it was the nonprofit research, training, and technical assistance affiliate of the National District Attorneys Association (NDAA). NDAA representatives regularly meet with the Department of Justice, Members of Congress, and other national associations to represent the views of prosecutors to influence federal and national policies and programs that affect law enforcement and prosecution.

[43] American Prosecutors Research Institute, *Exploring the Feasibility and Efficacy of Performance Measures in Prosecution and their Application to Community Prosecution* (2009).

[44] Department of Justice, Office of Community Oriented Policing Services (COPS), *Law Enforcement Tech Guide for Creating Performance Measures that Work*, (Feb. 5, 2007). The COPS office within DOJ partners with law enforcement, businesses, and other federal agencies to enhance policing activities and outcomes.

[45] Association of Prosecuting Attorneys, *A Framework for High Performance Prosecutorial Services*, 2011. DOJ's BJA provides leadership and services in grant administration and

criminal justice policy development to support local, state, and tribal justice strategies to achieve safer communities.

[46] Brennan Center for Justice, *Federal Prosecution for the 21st Century*, (September 23, 2014). The Brennan Center for Justice at New York University School of Law is a nonpartisan law and policy institute that seeks to improve our systems of democracy and justice. Department of Justice, Office of Justice Programs, Bureau of Justice Assistance, Center for Program Evaluation and Performance Management, *Measures of Community Prosecution Performance*, accessed February 3, 2015, https://www.bja.gov/evaluation/program-adjudication/comm-prosecution5.htm. The Center for Program Evaluation and Performance Measurement maintains online evaluation and performance measurement resources designed to assist state and local criminal justice planners and practitioners, among others.

[47] The Brennan Center notes that violent crime cases are resource intensive, and offices could therefore show fewer violent crime cases on their docket yet those cases may absorb a larger share of office resources. To better refine this measure, offices could collect data on the number of offices hours or percentage of budget spent on violent crime cases. Such a measure may be slightly more difficult to track, but would more accurately reflect whether resources were focused on violent cases.

[48] Although DOJ does not track this information, DOJ's Office of the Inspector General (OIG) published a report in 2011 in which it analyzed data available from DOJ and reported on petition review time frames and associated challenges. For example, the OIG reported that from the beginning of fiscal year 2005 through the end of fiscal year 2010, DOJ took an average of 14.5 months to process clemency petitions (petitions for commutation of sentence and pardon—9.8 months in OPA and 4.7 months in ODAG— and send them to the White House. DOJ, *Office of the Inspector General, Audit of the Department of Justice Processing of Clemency Petitions*, Audit Report 11-45 (Washington, D.C.: September 2011).

[49] OPA set targets related to (1) the number of clemency petitions it processes during a given fiscal year, and (2) the number of clemency petitions that remain pending within OPA at the end of the fiscal year. Given recent and potential future increases in petition filings, OPA increased its targets for processing petitions from 1,500 in fiscal year 2014 to 1,700 in fiscal year 2015, and 3,500 in fiscal year 2016. Similarly, OPA increased its targets for petitions pending within OPA from 1,800 at the end of fiscal year 2014 to 10,000 at the end of fiscal years 2015 and 2016. However, OPA reports that the number of petitions it can reasonably expect to process to completion during fiscal years 2015 and 2016 depends on the number of additional staff OPA is able to hire and how quickly they can be brought on board and trained.

[50] DOJ clarified in a written response from the ODAG that processing petitions "with all due speed" is its expectation and is the message that OPA sends to each of its staff.

[51] DOJ, Office of the Inspector General, *Audit of the Department of Justice Processing of Clemency Petitions*, Audit Report 11-45, (September 2011). Specifically, the OIG analyzed data available in DOJ's Executive Clemency Tracking System related to clemency petitions pending at the beginning of fiscal year 2005 and clemency petitions opened between the beginning of fiscal year 2005 and the end of fiscal year 2010.

[52] Project Management Institute, Inc. *The Standard for Program Management,* Third Edition, 2013.

[53] Program evaluations are individual systematic studies that assess the strengths and weaknesses of programs, policies, and organizations to improve their effectiveness. Program evaluation is different from performance measurement, which measures progress toward pre-

established goals but does not necessarily measure program effectiveness. BOP officials said they do not currently have operable metrics in place related to reentry for RSD because it continues to develop a bureau-wide reentry strategy and the existing metrics are suspended pending future revision or replacement. BOP officials told us they plan to complete their strategy by the end of calendar year 2015, at which point they will turn to the revision of existing (and potential development of new) related performance metrics.

[54] Bureau of Prisons, Reentry Services Division, *A Directory of Bureau of Prisons' National Programs*, (May 2014).

[55] BOP's Parenting Program provides inmates information and counseling through directed classes on how to enhance relationships with children even while incarcerated.

[56] BOP's Mental Health Step Down Program is a residential treatment program offering an intermediate level of care for inmates with serious mental illnesses.

[57] DOJ's National Institute of Justice, its research arm, notes the importance of ensuring that studies used to determine if programs are effective address the same program model and not similar program models that may vary in important ways.

[58] The 3 BOP programs include (1) the Federal Prison Industries Program, which employs and provides job skills training to inmates; (2) the Residential Drug Treatment Program (RDAP), which provides intensive cognitive-behavioral drug abuse treatment; and (3) the Bureau Rehabilitation and Values Enhancement (BRAVE) program, which is designed to facilitate favorable institutional adjustment and reduce incidents of misconduct for young male offenders. The three corresponding BOP evaluations are (1) BOP, *PREP: Training Inmates through Industrial Work Participation, and Vocational and Apprenticeship Instruction*, (September 1996); (2) BOP, Office of Research and Evaluation, *TRIAD Drug Treatment Evaluation Project Final Report of Three-Year Outcomes: Part 1*, (September 2000); (3) BOP, Office of Research and Evaluation, *Technical Report for the Results from the Evaluation of the First Two Years of the Beckley Responsibility and Values Enhancement (BRAVE) Program*, (BOP estimates report completion in 2001). In addition, BOP currently has plans to evaluate a fourth program—BOP's Sex Offender Treatment Program—to examine the program's impact on recidivism.

[59] GAO, *State and Federal Prisoners: Profiles of Inmate Characteristics in 1991 and 1997*, GAO/GGD-00-117, (Washington, D.C.: May 2000).

[60] DOJ, Office of Justice Programs (OJP), BJS, *Compendium of Federal Justice Statistics, 1997*, (October 1999). DOJ, OJP, BJS, *Federal Justice Statistics, 2012–Statistical Tables*, (January 2015). Data we use from these reports are "as of" the last day of the relevant fiscal year (September 30, 1997; and September 30, 2012).

[61] We previously recommended that BOP develop a plan to carry out future evaluations of BOP's psychology treatment programs. BOP concurred with this recommendation, and in January 2015, BOP provided us with an evaluation plan to address this recommendation. GAO, *Bureau of Prisons: Timelier Reviews, Plan for Evaluations, and Updated Policies Could Improve Inmate Mental Health Services Oversight,* GAO-13-1 (Washington, D.C.: July 2013).

[62] Specifically, BOP plans to conduct annual assessments of program fidelity (a form of process evaluation that assesses the extent to which programs are implemented as intended) for all 9 programs. Additionally, through fiscal year 2022, BOP intends to perform short-term outcome evaluations for 4 of 9 programs. According to BOP, short-term evaluations may be as simple as a pre/post knowledge test, an exercise to demonstrate acquired skills, or an evaluation project that more closely resembles a traditional research project. BOP also intends to measure long-term evaluation outcomes for 1 of 9 programs—its Residential Sex

Offender Treatment Program. According to the plan, BOP intends to evaluate the program's impact on recidivism.

[63] For instance, officials explained that when BOP performed its evaluation of the Residential Drug Abuse Treatment Program in the 1990s, they were able to draw both a treatment group (inmates who participated in RDAP) and a comparison group (inmates who qualified for RDAP but did not participate in it) from among BOP inmates. However, since that study, BOP has made RDAP available to all inmates who qualify for it—making it difficult to draw a comparison group from among BOP inmates. Nevertheless, a BOP official said BOP is examining the feasibility of identifying a comparison group using inmates who qualified for RDAP but who did not have the opportunity to participate because, in certain cases, their sentence completion date arrived prior to the chance to enroll.

[64] For instance, statistical procedures, such as "propensity score analysis," can be used to statistically model variables that influence participants' assigned to a program compared with individuals not assigned. These procedures are then applied to the analysis of outcome data to reduce the influence of those variables on the results attributable to the program. In BOP's evaluation of its Federal Prison Industries program, it used propensity scoring to select matched comparison group members. BOP, *PREP: Training Inmates through Industrial Work Participation, and Vocational Apprenticeship Instruction,* (September 1996). Additionally, BOP plans to use this method in its planned evaluation of the Residential Sex Offender Treatment Program. For more on designing evaluations, see GAO, *Designing Evaluations: 2012 Revision*, GAO-12-208G (Washington, D.C.: January 2012).

[65] American Evaluation Association, *An Evaluation Roadmap for a More Effective Government,* (Revised October 2013).

[66] GAO-06-15. We did not include the remaining five key practices for two reasons. First, our prior work on key collaborative efforts has typically focused on collaborative efforts among multiple departments and agencies making those practices less relevant to DOJ's efforts, which are largely internal. Second, DOJ's internal initiative is in its early stages, and we have generally discussed the remaining key collaboration practices for those interagency collaboration efforts that have been under way for some time.

[67] The Violence Reduction Network is a federal law enforcement partnership with five high-crime cities and their local law enforcement entities: Camden, New Jersey; Chicago, Illinois; Detroit, Michigan; Oakland/Richmond, California; and Wilmington, Delaware. Through this partnership, DOJ components such as ATF, DEA, FBI, USMS, and EOUSA work with police chiefs and city leaders, among others, to develop ways to make progress on each city's violence reduction strategies. This work includes sharing federal resources with the cities, such as access to databases, training, and other technical resources.

[68] The $173 million was not a request to increase funding from the previous fiscal year, but rather to sustain the previous year's level of funding and redistribute the funding to support the Smart on Crime Initiative, DOJ was ultimately appropriated $122 million of the $173 million for fiscal year 2015.

[69] For example, one United States Attorney district noted in its action plan that it held a meeting in August 2014 with the district's federal law enforcement agencies to address the Smart on Crime Initiative.

[70] Congress appropriated funds at the requested levels for both BOP and the Offices of the United States Attorneys.

## End Notes for Appendix I

[1] Our prior work establishes 9 key attributes of successful performance measures. GAO, *Tax Administration: IRS Needs to Further Refine Its Tax Filing Season Performance Measures,* GAO-03-143 (Washington, D.C.: November 2002).

[2] The 6 attributes not included in this review are objectivity, reliability, core program activities, limited overlap, balance, and government-wide priorities. For more information about these key attributes, see GAO-03-143.

[3] GAO, *Information Sharing: DHS Could Better Define How It Plans to Meet Its State and Local Mission and Improve Performance Accountability,* GAO-11-223 (Washington, D.C.: December 2010).

[4] Project Management Institute, Inc., *The Standard for Program Management,* 2013.

[5] American Evaluation Association, *An Evaluation Roadmap for a More Effective Government,* (revised October 2013).

[6] GAO, *Results-Oriented Government: Practices That Can Help Enhance and Sustain Collaboration among Federal Agencies*, GAO-06-15 (Washington, D.C.: Oct. 21, 2005); *Managing for Results: Key Considerations for Implementing Interagency Collaborative Mechanisms,* GAO-12-1022 (Washington, D.C.: Sept. 27, 2012); and *Managing for Results: Implementation Approaches Used to Enhance Collaboration in Interagency Groups*, GAO-14-220 (Washington, D.C: Feb. 14, 2014.

[7] The five key practices not included in this review are reinforcing agency accountability for collaborative efforts through agency plans and reports; reinforcing individual accountability for collaborative efforts through performance management systems; developing mechanisms to monitor, evaluate, and report on results; establishing compatible policies, procedures, and other means to operate across agency boundaries; and defining and articulating a common outcome.

In: Challenges to the Federal Prison System ... ISBN: 978-1-63484-236-5
Editor: Bryan M. Walker 

*Chapter 2*

# OFFENDER REENTRY: CORRECTIONAL STATISTICS, REINTEGRATION INTO THE COMMUNITY, AND RECIDIVISM*

*Nathan James*

## SUMMARY

The number of people incarcerated in the United States grew steadily for nearly 30 years. That number has been slowly decreasing since 2008, but as of 2012 there were still over 2 million people incarcerated in prisons and jails across the country. The Bureau of Justice Statistics (BJS) reports that since 1990 an average of 590,400 inmates have been released annually from state and federal prisons and almost 5 million ex offenders are under some form of community-based supervision.

Nearly all prisoners will return to their communities as some point. Offender reentry can include all the activities and programming conducted to prepare prisoners to return safely to the community and to live as law-abiding citizens. Some ex-offenders, however, eventually end up back in prison. The BJS's most recent study on recidivism showed that within five years of release nearly three-quarters of ex-offenders released in 2005 came back into contact with the criminal justice system, and more than half returned to prison after either being convicted for a new

---

* This is an edited, reformatted and augmented version of a Congressional Research Service publication RL34287, prepared for Members and Committees of Congress, dated January 12, 2015.

crime or for violating the conditions of their release. Compared with the average American, ex-offenders are less educated, less likely to be gainfully employed, and more likely to have a history of mental illness or substance abuse—all of which have been shown to be risk factors for recidivism.

Three phases are associated with offender reentry programs: programs that take place during incarceration, which aim to prepare offenders for their eventual release; programs that take place during offenders' release period, which seek to connect ex-offenders with the various services they may require; and long-term programs that take place as ex-offenders permanently reintegrate into their communities, which attempt to provide offenders with support and supervision. There is a wide array of offender reentry program designs, and these programs can differ significantly in range, scope, and methodology. Researchers in the offender reentry field have suggested that the best programs begin during incarceration and extend throughout the release and reintegration process. Despite the relative lack of highly rigorous research on the effectiveness of some reentry programs, an emerging "what works" literature suggests that programs focusing on work training and placement, drug and mental health treatment, and housing assistance have proven to be effective.

The federal government's involvement in offender reentry programs typically occurs through grant funding, which is available through a wide array of federal programs at the Departments of Justice, Labor, Education, and Health and Human Services. However, only a handful of grant programs in the federal government are designed explicitly for offender reentry purposes. The Department of Justice has started an interagency Reentry Council to coordinate federal reentry efforts and advance effective reentry policies.

The Second Chance Act (P.L. 110-199) was enacted on April 9, 2008. The act expanded the existing offender reentry grant program at the Department of Justice and created a wide array of targeted grant-funded pilot programs.

## BACKGROUND

Over 95% of the prison population today will be released at some point in the future.[1] Since 1990, an average of 590,400 inmates have been released annually from state and federal prisons.[2] The Department of Justice's (DOJ's) Bureau of Justice Statistics (BJS) has estimated that nearly three-quarters of all released prisoners will be rearrested within five years of their release and about 6 in 10 will be reconvicted.[3] Many studies have indicated that reentry initiatives that combine work training and placement with counseling and housing assistance can reduce recidivism rates.[4] According to the BJS, the average per prisoner cost of incarceration in state prison in 2010 was approximately $28,000 per year.[5] States collectively spent nearly $48.5 billion on their correctional systems in 2010, the most recent year for which data are available.[6]

Offender reentry includes all the activities and programming conducted to prepare ex-convicts to return safely to the community and to live as law-abiding citizens. Reentry programs are typically divided into three phases: programs that prepare offenders to reenter society while they are in prison, programs that connect ex-offenders with services immediately after they are released from prison, and programs that provide long-term support and supervision for ex-offenders as they settle into communities permanently. Offender reentry programs vary widely in range, scope, and methodology. The best-designed programs, according to the research in the field, are those that span all three phases.[7]

## Correctional System Statistics

To understand the issue of offender reentry, one must first understand the ways in which ex-offenders are released into the community. It is also worthwhile to analyze the population of individuals serving sentences in correctional facilities, because the number of offenders reentering the community is necessarily related to the number and type of offenders serving prison sentences. This section analyzes national data on the nation's correctional system.

### Population in Correctional Facilities

The correctional system includes two main forms of detention: jails and prisons. Jails, also known as local lockups, are facilities generally used to temporarily detain individuals who have been arrested or charged with a crime but not usually convicted.[8] The jail population is thus extremely fluid, with individuals usually staying for a matter of weeks, and includes individuals who may never be convicted of a crime. Prisons, on the other hand, typically house individuals who have been convicted of a crime and sentenced to a term of one year or longer. For this reason, the prison population is less fluid than the jail population.

The number of inmates incarcerated in correctional facilities steadily increased between 2000 and 2008 when it reached its peak of nearly 2.4 million inmates. However, in recent years the number of incarcerated individuals has declined. The number of inmates in prisons and local jails decreased by 15,400 (-0.7%) inmates in 2009; 21,900 (-1.0%) inmates in 2010; 30,400 (-1.3%) inmates in 2011; 11,300 (-0.5%) in 2012; and 9,000 (-0.4%) in 2013. The decrease in the correctional population in 2009 was the result of a declining jail population, but in 2010 and 2011, there was a decrease in the number of inmates held in both jails and prisons. The overall correctional population decreased again in 2012, but this was the result of a decline in the number of inmates held in prison; the number of inmates held in jails increased. While there was a decrease in the number of people incarcerated again in 2013, the number of people incarcerated in prisons actually increased between 2012 and 2013. The increase in the number of people incarcerated in prisons was offset by a decrease in the number of people incarcerated in jails. *Figure 1* shows the number of inmates incarcerated in the United States from 2000 to 2013 (the most recent data available).

Given the fact that 95% of all inmates will eventually return to the community,[9] the prison population has a direct impact on offender reentry. As the prison population grows, increasing numbers of ex-offenders are released from correctional facilities. Most of these ex-offenders are required to undergo some form of community supervision as part of their release. The following section explores the mechanisms and statistics surrounding the release of prisoners into the community.

## Offenders under Community Supervision

Ex-offenders can be released into the community through a variety of different mechanisms. Some offenders never serve prison sentences and instead serve their sentence on probation in their communities under supervision. Others serve most of their sentences in correctional facilities but are then released on parole to finish their sentences in their communities under supervision. Lastly, some offenders serve out their entire sentences in correctional facilities and are released unconditionally into the community.

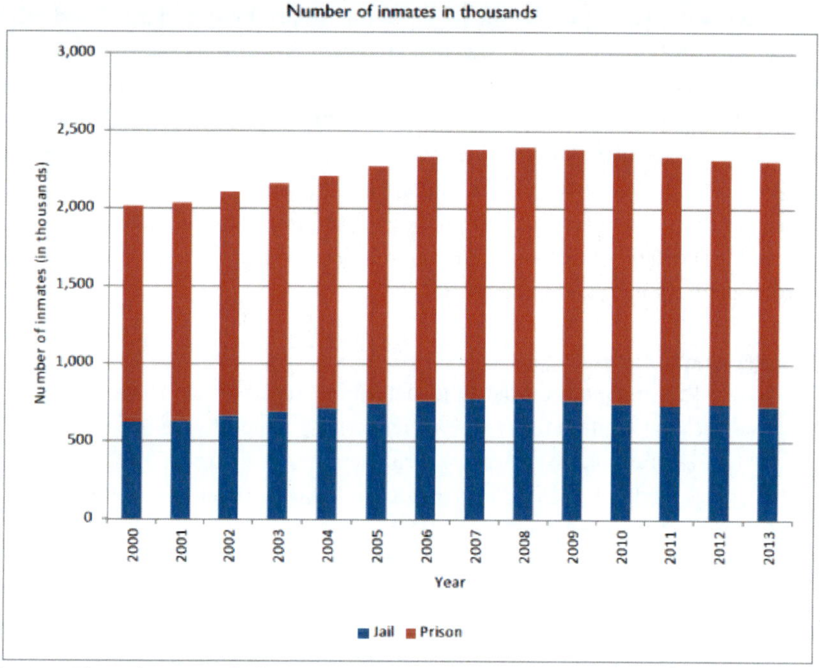


Source: The prison population counts were taken from U.S. Department of Justice, Office of Justice Programs, Bureau of Justice Statistics, Prisoners in 2011 and Prisoners in 2013. The jail population counts were taken from U.S. Department of Justice, Office of Justice Programs, Bureau of Justice Statistics, Jail Inmates and Midyear 2013– Statistical Tables.

Figure 1. Number of Inmates Incarcerated in the United States, 2000-2013.

### *Probation*

Individuals who are found guilty of committing a crime that is deemed not serious enough for imprisonment can be sentenced to serve their sentences under community supervision (probation). Offenders on probation typically must adhere to certain conditions and check in regularly with their probation officers. Violation of these conditions or failure to appear before their probation officers can lead to further criminal sanctions, including incarceration. In some instances, offenders can be sentenced to a mixed term of prison and probation.

### Parole

Individuals who have served most of their sentences in a correctional facility are sometimes eligible to complete their sentences in the community under conditional supervision. While some states have a parole system in place, Congress abolished parole at the federal level effective November 1, 1987. However, there is a small percentage of federal offenders who were sentenced prior to November 1, 1987, who are still eligible for parole. The conditions associated with parole can vary from case to case, but typically include drug testing and regular contact with a parole officer. Violations of these conditions can result in the parolee returning to prison to serve out the remaining portion of his or her sentence. There are two different kinds of parole: discretionary and mandatory.

### Discretionary Parole

States that use parole boards to determine whether a prisoner should be released into the community have discretionary parole. Parole boards have the authority to conditionally release a prisoner into the community based on a statutory or an administrative determination that the prisoner is eligible.

### Mandatory Parole

States that have statutory language determining when offenders should be released into the community have mandatory parole. Jurisdictions that use determinate sentencing[10] often include provisions specifying when inmates should be conditionally released from prison after serving a specified portion of their original sentences.

*Figure 2* shows the number of offenders who were supervised in the community, either through probation or through parole, during the period from 2000 to 2013 (the most recent data available). The data show that the majority of offenders on community supervision are on probation (84%, on average, between 2000 and 2013). Also, trends in the number of people on community supervision mirror those of incarceration. The total number of people on community supervision peaked in 2007 (compared to the number of people incarcerated, which peaked in 2008) and it has been declining since. The decline in the total number of people on community supervision has largely been driven by a decline in the number of people on probation. The number of people on parole has actually increased since 2007, which might reflect the fact that a number of inmates who were sentenced to terms of incarceration in the 1990s and early 2000s are now being released on parole.

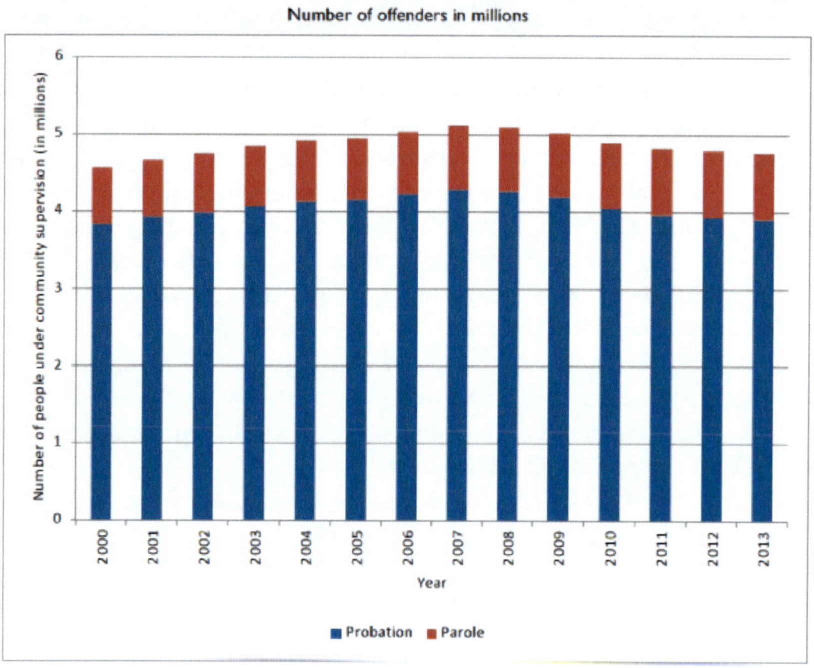


Source: The number of probationers and parolees were taken from U.S. Department of Justice, Office of Justice Programs, Bureau of Justice Statistics, Probation and Parole in the United States, 2013.

Figure 2. Number of Offenders Under Community Supervision, 2000-2013.

The relationship between the prison and parole populations is an important one for a number of reasons. Offenders serving their sentences in prison have generally committed more serious crimes than offenders who serve their sentences in jail or on probation; as previously noted, the prison population typically includes individuals sentenced to more than a year of incarceration. Parolees, meanwhile, often return to the community after a prolonged period of incarceration and usually face a period of adjustment.

## Recidivism

Recidivism is often defined as the rearrest, reconviction, or reincarceration of an ex-offender within a given time frame. As a result of this broad definition of recidivism, most studies include technical violations of an offender's parole or probation (such as failing a drug test or not showing up for a meeting, for example) within their general recidivism statistics. Rearrest statistics also include individuals who are found not guilty of the charges. For these reasons, some studies have focused on reincarceration with a new prison sentence as a more accurate recidivism statistic, arguing that technical violations are really an extension of an offender's original prison term and not a newly committed crime. Essentially, there are two competing philosophies about what recidivism should mean.[11] On the one hand are those who argue that any new contact with the criminal justice system, no matter how minor, should be considered recidivism on the part of an ex-offender. On the other hand are those who argue that recidivism should be more narrowly defined as the commission of a new crime, resulting in a new sentence, by an ex-offender. What one includes in the definition of recidivism has a substantial impact on the rate of recidivism reported.

Regardless of what definition is used, recidivism is a difficult subject to study. Tracking recidivism involves following the cases of individuals for a number of years and relying on state or national-level data sets that contain inherent inaccuracies. For example, if an offender is released in California but commits a new crime in Maine, the researchers must be able to match those two records together to make a definitive statement about recidivism. This match is typically done by consulting the FBI's master database of convictions; however, as we will see later, this database contains omissions that may affect the results of recidivism studies. A number of studies have been conducted on this issue, and most states have calculated their own recidivism rates. However, for the sake of providing the most comprehensive overview of recidivism, this section focuses on the most recently conducted national-level study.

### *Bureau of Justice Statistics 2005 Recidivism Study*

The Bureau of Justice Statistics (BJS) study on the recidivism of a cohort of inmates released in 1994 was, at the time, one of the most comprehensive national-level recidivism studies ever conducted.[12] The BJS recently published a new report that examined the recidivism rates for 404,638 prisoners released in 30 states for five years after their release from prison in 2005.[13] The prisoners included in the study represent approximately three-quarters of the inmates released in 2005. The 2005 BJS recidivism study used a larger sample and a longer follow-up period than the 1994 study.[14]

Data show that by the end of the five-year follow-up period, approximately three-quarters (76.6%) of prisoners released in 2005 were rearrested. Furthermore, the BJS found that most released prisoners were rearrested within one year of being released. By the end of the first year following release, 43.4% of inmates were rearrested. The longer released prisoners went without being rearrested, the less likely they were to be rearrested. As shown in *Figure 3*, compared to the arrest rate of 43.4% in the first year, 28.5% released prisoners who were not arrested in the first year were arrested for the first time in the second year after release. The proportion of released prisoners who were arrested for the first time over the course of the last three years of the follow-up period continued to decrease.

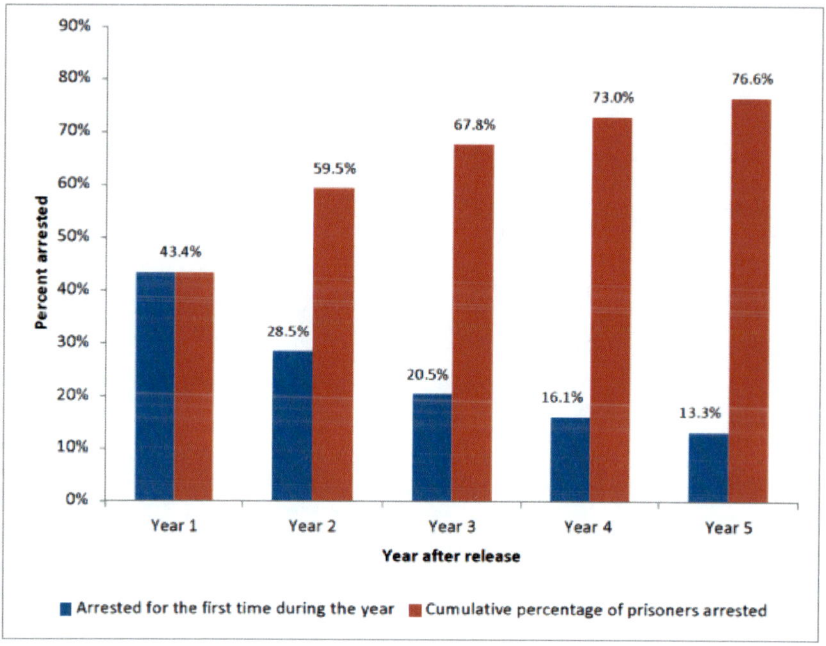


Source: U.S. Department of Justice, Office of Justice Programs, Bureau of Justice Statistics, Recidivism of Prisoners Released in 30 States in 2005: Patterns from 2005 to 2010.

Notes: The denominators for the proportion of released prisoners arrested for the first time during the year were 404,638 for year one; 229,035 for year two; 163,679 for year three; 130,128 for year four; and 109,186 for year five. The numerators include released prisoners who were arrested during the year who had not been arrested since release.

Figure 3. Proportion of Released Prisoners Arrested for the First Time at the End of the Year and Cumulative Percentage of Released Prisoners Rearrested.

Data show that a greater proportion of released property offenders were rearrested than violent, drug, and public order offenders (see *Figure 4*). By the end of the five year follow-up period, 82.1% of released property offenders were rearrested, compared to 76.9% of drug offenders, 73.6% of public order offenders, and 71.3% of violent offenders. Data show that the general pattern of recidivism shown in *Figure 3* continued regardless of the offenses for which released prisoners were incarcerated. Most released offenders, regardless of their offense, were likely to be rearrested within one year of being released and the increase in the proportion of rearrested prisoners started to slow the longer prisoners had been out of prison.

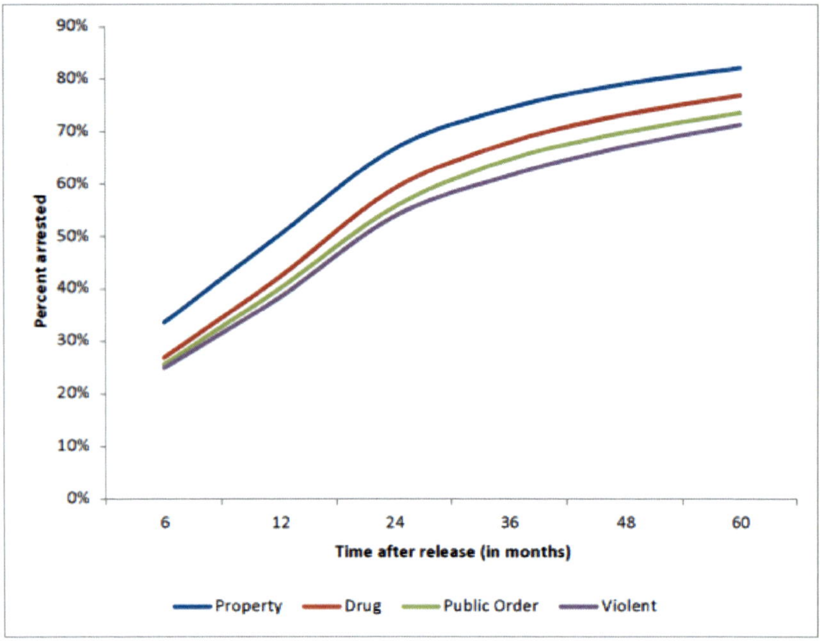


Source: U.S. Department of Justice, Office of Justice Programs, Bureau of Justice Statistics, Recidivism of Prisoners Released in 30 States in 2005: Patterns from 2005 to 2010.

Figure 4. Proportion of Released Prisoners Rearrested, by Offense Type.

The BJS also found that prisoners with longer criminal histories were more likely to be rearrested within five years of being released. Data show that 86.5% of released prisoners with 10 or more prior arrests were rearrested within five years (see *Figure 5*). In comparison, 60.8% of released prisoners with four or fewer prior arrests and 75.9% of released prisoners with five to nine prior arrests were rearrested within five years.

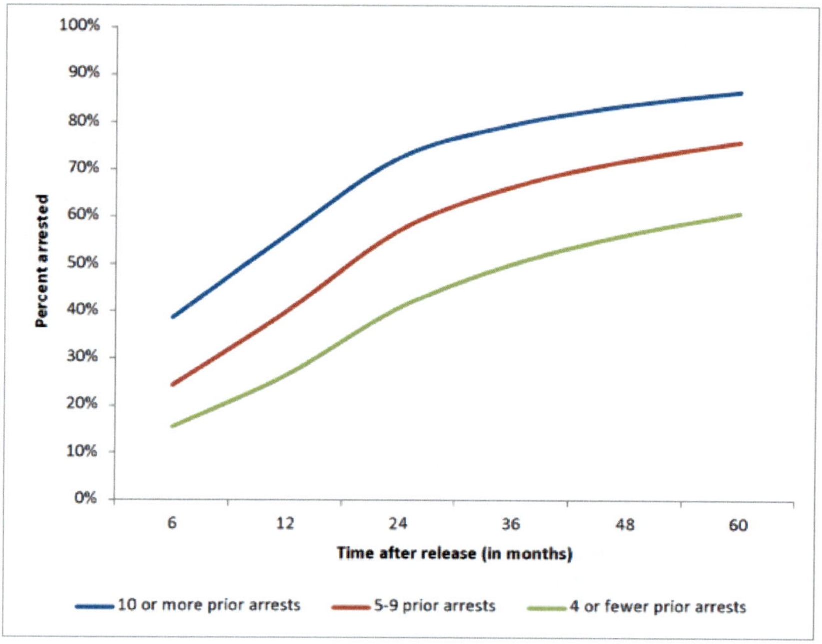


Source: U.S. Department of Justice, Office of Justice Programs, Bureau of Justice Statistics, Recidivism of Prisoners Released in 30 States in 2005: Patterns from 2005 to 2010.

Figure 5. Proportion of Released Prisoners Rearrested, by Criminal History.

As previously discussed, the definition of "recidivism" can affect measured recidivism. The data from the BJS study bear this out. Arrest is the broadest definition of recidivism, and when this definition is used it produces the highest measured recidivism (see *Figure 6*). More restrictive definitions of recidivism result in lower measured recidivism. For example, 76.6% of prisoners released in 2005 were rearrested within five years, but 60.0% were adjudicated,[15] 55.4% were convicted for a new crime, 55.1% were returned to prison,[16] 44.9% were incarcerated,[17] and 28.2% were imprisoned.[18]

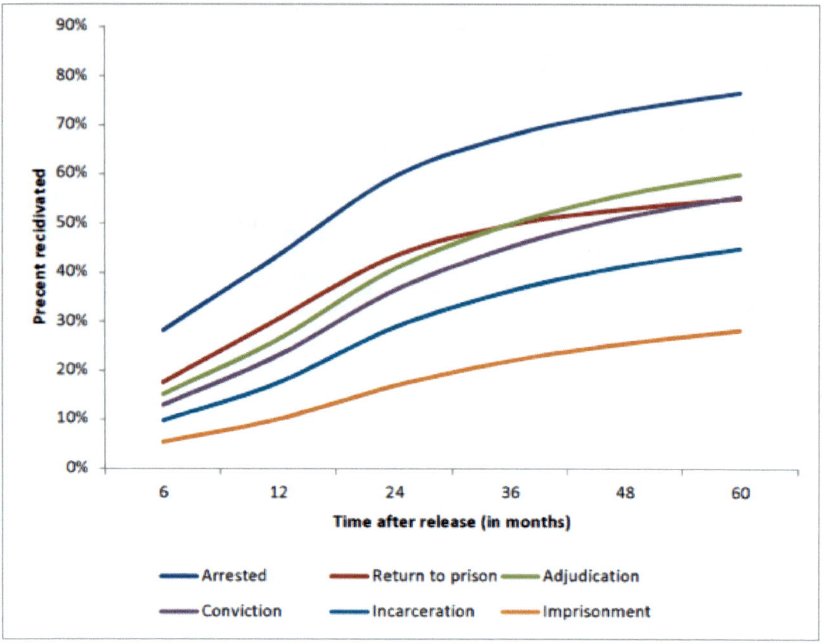


Source: U.S. Department of Justice, Office of Justice Programs, Bureau of Justice Statistics, Recidivism of Prisoners Released in 30 States in 2005: Patterns from 2005 to 2010.

Notes: "Adjudication" refers to arrests that resulted in a subsequent court adjudication or disposition (e.g., convictions, dismissals, acquittals, or deferred adjudications). "Conviction" refers to arrests that resulted in a subsequent court conviction. "Incarceration" refers to arrests that resulted in a prison or jail sentence. "Imprisonment" refers to arrests that resulted in a prison sentence. "Return to prison" refers to arrests that resulted in a conviction with a disposition of a prison sentence or when prisoners were returned to prison without a new conviction due to technical violations of the terms of their release.

Figure 6. Measured Recidivism Based on Different Definitions of Recidivism.

### *Limitations of Recidivism Statistics*

The data used in the BJS come from official records maintained by the states' and the Federal Bureau of Investigation's (FBI's) official criminal history repositories. These repositories understate the actual recidivism levels to some unknown extent because they rely on local police agencies and courts to supply them with notifying documents. These documents are not always filed by local police departments or courts, however. In addition, if the offender provided a different name or a fraudulent identity document to police, and this misinformation was not discovered, they would likely not be captured by the data. Lastly, even if the criminal is correctly identified and the document is sent to the repository, the repository may not be able to match the person identified in the document with their records. This could occur, for example, if the document that has been submitted is filled out incorrectly or is illegible.

Moreover, as previously noted, there is some debate about what kind of outcome measure should be included when measuring recidivism. Should recidivism statistics include any contact with the criminal justice system by an ex-offender? Or should recidivism statistics be limited to the commission of crimes by ex-offenders that result in new convictions or new sentences? The BJS study showed wide differentials between general recidivism, which includes any contact with the criminal justice system, and re-conviction rates for new crimes. The length of the follow-up period will also play a role in the recidivism statistics that are generated. The BJS study shows that recidivism, no matter how recidivism is measured, continues to climb, albeit at a decreasing rate, as the length of the follow-up period increases.

For all of these reasons, caution should be taken when attempting to draw conclusions about the efficacy of policy measures based solely on recidivism statistics. When using recidivism statistics to evaluate a program, it is important to understand exactly what is included in the definition of recidivism. For example, consider the following hypothetical scenario: a program is evaluated and shows significant decreases in the number of ex-offenders that are convicted of new crimes and sentenced to new prison terms; however, the number of ex-offenders arrested for violating their parole actually increased. Was this program successful or not? Did it make society safer or not? This may well be an unlikely scenario, but it calls attention to the fact that recidivism may mean different things to different people. While recidivism statistics remain the best information available concerning whether ex-offenders come into contact with the criminal justice system after being released from prison and what the nature of that contact is, they are but one factor to be considered when evaluating the efficacy of a program, because of the concerns outlined above.

## OFFENDER REENTRY: A BRIEF LITERATURE REVIEW

The vast majority of prisoners currently being detained in secure facilities will, someday, be released into the community, and more offenders are transitioning into the community today than ever before. Offender reentry is a complex issue that touches on a wide range of social and governmental networks and programs. Offender reentry policies can vary significantly from state to state, and from community to community within particular states. The policies affecting prisoners and the kinds of programs available to them both in and out of prison depend on a variety of factors, including the availability of funding for social programs within states and communities and the number of private nonprofit and religious organizations operating in a given community. The federal government plays a supporting role through the numerous grant funding opportunities (discussed below). Complicating factors affecting how offender reentry works in a given community can include

- the varying types of sentences handed down,
- the different kinds of release mechanisms available to judges,
- the types of programs provided in prisons by correctional systems,
- the intensity of supervision provided or required by the parole or releasing agency,
- the family and community support available to the offender,
- the kinds of social services available in the offender's community, and
- the status of the local economy and the offender's ability to obtain employment.[19]

## Offender Reentry Defined

Before any discussion of offender reentry programs, however, it is useful to comment on what constitutes offender reentry. Some observers note that offender reentry is the natural byproduct of incarceration, because all prisoners who are not sentenced to life in prison and who do not die in prison will reenter the community at some point. According to this school of thought, reentry is not a program or some kind of legal status but rather a process that almost all offenders will undergo.[20] A variant on this approach to reentry is the concept that offender reentry, "simply defined, includes all activities and programming conducted to prepare ex-convicts to return safely to the community and to live as law abiding citizens."[21] The basic idea here is that every activity and process that a prisoner undergoes while in the judicial and correctional systems will have some nexus with their reentry into the community.

Although this broad definition of reentry certainly encompasses all the activities that may impinge on or affect a prisoner's reentry into society, it may be a cumbersome one for the purposes of crafting and evaluating government policies. For example, it is difficult, if not impossible, to measure the outcome of a reentry program if one includes in the definition of reentry every activity that a prisoner undergoes during his time in the criminal justice system. This has led many in the field to focus on a more narrow and thus more manageable definition of reentry. This more narrow definition is often stated in two parts: correctional programs that focus on the transition to the community (such as prerelease, work release, halfway houses, or other programs specifically aiming at reentry) and programs that have initiated some form of treatment (such as substance abuse, life skills, education, or mental health) in prison that is linked to community programs that will continue the treatment once the prisoner has been released.[22] Narrowing the definition of reentry thusly allows policy makers to focus on programs that expressly aim to manage the transition from detention to the community.

## Program Effectiveness: The "What Works" Literature

Compared with other social science fields, there has been a relative lack of rigorously designed studies on the issue of offender reentry. Nevertheless, in recent years, there has been increasing attention on this issue and a number of new studies have been published. This has allowed academics to undertake some of the first broad meta-analyses[23] of offender reentry studies. Some of these studies have hewn closely to the "what works" paradigm created by University of Maryland researchers for a National Institute of Justice report to Congress.[24] This concept was adapted to the field of offender reentry in a 2003 St. Louis University Study.[25] The "what works" literature attempts to identify programs that are effective by creating a scoring system to evaluate studies based on whether they can be proven to have an impact. Inherent to this approach is the need to identify program evaluations that provide evidence concerning the effect the program had on certain outcome measures. The "what works" paradigm essentially focuses on whether studies have accomplished the following things:

- controlled for variables in their analysis that may have been the underlying cause of any observed connection between the program being studied and the outcome measures being analyzed;

- determined whether there are measurement errors resulting from problems with the study, including such things as participants being lost over time or low response rates to interview requests; and
- calculated the statistical power of the analysis to detect the program's effects on outcome measures. Included in this category are things such as sample size and the base rate of crime in the community.[26]

The "what works" model uses these core criteria to place studies into five distinct categories, with category 5 being the most scientifically rigorous, and thus considered most effective, studies. The model then uses these criteria to identify programs that, based on the evidence considered, have been proven to work, programs that are promising, and programs that do not work.

The National Reentry Resource Center (NRRC), in collaboration with the Urban Institute (UI), developed the What Works in Reentry Clearinghouse (Clearinghouse). The Clearinghouse provides access to research on the effectiveness of a variety of reentry programs and practices.[27] The criteria established by the UI for which studies would be included in the Clearinghouse closely hew to the "what works" model. First, in order for a study to be included in the Clearinghouse it must evaluate whether a particular program, practice, or policy improves reentry outcomes for returning prisoners and the effect of the intervention on at least one of a number of relevant outcomes (e.g., recidivism, substance use, housing, employment, and mental health). If these criteria are met, then the study must also satisfy the following minimum set of standards in terms of methodological rigor:

- The study must employ either random assignment or quasi-experimental methods with matched groups or statistical controls for differences between groups.
- The sample size must be at least 30 individuals in both the treatment and comparison groups.
- The study must have either been conducted by an independent researcher or published in a peer-reviewed journal.

***Employment***

The conventional wisdom is that post-release employment is one of the most important elements for an ex-offender to successfully transition back into the community.[28] Released prisoners frequently identify employment as one of the most important factors in their efforts to stay crime-free after incarceration.

While studies have shown that employment can aid in preventing recidivism, in general, research on the relationship between participation in employment programs and recidivism has yielded mixed results. The Clearinghouse included five studies that examined the effects of programs that provided job training and/or post-release employment services for prisoners. Of these five studies, only two found that the program helped reduce recidivism, though neither program had a significant effect on post-release employment. Another program had a positive effect on helping released prisoners find post-incarceration employment, though this program did not have an effect on recidivism. Research on the effect of work release programs was mixed; half of the six studies in the Clearinghouse found that work release program either reduced recidivism or helped prisoners find post-release employment while the other half did not. A majority of the research found that prisoners who participated in prison industries had lower levels of recidivism.

### *Substance Abuse Treatment*

For many prisoners who recently returned to their communities, substance abuse is often closely related to their difficulties with housing, employment, and mental health.[29] Generally, research in the Clearinghouse indicates that substance abuse treatment can help reduce recidivism and substance abuse amongst program participants, especially if the substance abuse treatment is provided in a therapeutic community (TC) setting.[30] There were 16 studies in the Clearinghouse that evaluated the effectiveness of TC substance abuse treatment, and most indicated that program participation had a positive effect on both recidivism and substance abuse. Research also suggests that aftercare can help promote positive outcomes for program participants, but these results could have been affected by selection bias. A majority of studies that evaluated non-TC substance abuse programs found either strong to moderate evidence that the programs reduced recidivism.

### *Education*

Educational credentials are increasingly important in order to obtain employment in a more competitive global economy. However, many prisoners have low levels of educational attainment. To help prepare prisoners for the workforce after they leave prison, many correctional facilities offer educational programs, including adult basic education (ABE), high school or GED programs, college or post-secondary programs, and vocational training.[31] Research included in the Clearinghouse show that post-secondary education had a strong effect on reducing recidivism, while there was a more modest effect for ABE programs. Studies of GED programs show that participants were no less likely to recidivate than non-participants. However, it is difficult to draw any definitive conclusions about the effectiveness of any of these programs because there were a limited number of studies that met the criteria for inclusion.[32] There was more research on vocational education programs, but the findings from these studies were mixed. The research on vocational education programs suggests that the quality of the program may be an important factor in achieving reductions in recidivism.

### *Mental Health*

A significant number of prisoners have problems with mental illness, and these problems might co-occur with a substance abuse or a physical health problem.[33] Research on the effectiveness of prison-based mental health treatment suggests that these programs can help reduce recidivism. The Clearinghouse includes four studies that evaluated programs that offered a continuity of care approach, and all four found significant reductions in recidivism amongst participants.[34] Evaluations of three other programs that focus on cognition and mental well-being, but which are not focused on prisoners with a diagnosed mental illness, suggest that these "curriculum-based" treatment programs can help reduce recidivism. For example, a program that provided 70 weeks of classes (including a phase that incorporates a cognitive-behavioral approach) that focused on problem solving, goal setting, managing stress and fear, and improving cognitive skills, was found to have a positive effect on recidivism.

### *Housing*

Acquiring housing is a challenge that most individuals face soon after leaving prison. Obtaining housing is complicated by several factors, including the scarcity of affordable and available housing, legal barriers, discrimination against ex-offenders, and strict eligibility requirements for federally subsidized housing.[35] Like many other reentry programs, the research on the effect of halfway houses on recidivism is mixed. There were three studies in the Clearinghouse that evaluated the effectiveness of halfway housing programs. Two of the studies found that the programs had no effect on recidivism. However, the most methodologically rigorous of the three studies suggests that halfway houses can reduce recidivism. The effect of halfway housing programs on recidivism appears to be largely determined by a participant's level of risk to recidivate (participants that are at a higher level of risk to recidivate are more likely to benefit) and by the quality of the particular program.[36]

### *Limitations of the "What Works" Literature*

A review of the research in the Clearinghouse shows that there is a dearth of high-quality research on the effectiveness of many reentry programs. While there were 16 studies on the effectiveness of TC-based substance abuse treatment that were methodologically rigorous enough to be included in the Clearinghouse, there was only one study of an ABE program, two studies of GED programs, and three studies of halfway houses. The lack of a robust body of literature on the effectiveness of some reentry programs can make it difficult to determine whether a program is indeed effective.

It is important to note here that just because a program has been reported to work in one location, or for a certain population, does not necessarily mean that it can be just as effective in other locations or among other populations. A number of factors can impinge on a program's effectiveness in any given location. For example, while knowing that a program has worked in the past can provide a model or blueprint to guide policy practitioners in other locations, how a program is implemented is just as important to its ultimate success as the underlying model that it is based on. The most effective model program can be compromised if it is not implemented properly. In addition, geographic, demographic, and other differences between locations can affect whether a program that succeeded in one place succeeds in another. Nevertheless, knowing that a program has worked in the past is of use to policy makers as they consider where to allocate funding and other resources.

### *Conclusion*

After reviewing the available literature, some patterns appear to emerge. Many of the programs that have been proven to be effective share some of the same attributes, regardless of whether they focus on vocational training, substance abuse prevention, mental health services, or obtaining housing. The attributes shared by most of these programs include the following:

- they start during institutional placement, but take place mostly in the community;
- they are intensive in nature, lasting typically at least six months;
- they focus services on individuals determined to be at high risk of recidivating through the use of risk-assessment classifications; and

- if they are treatment programs, they use cognitive-behavioral treatment techniques, matching particular therapists and programs to the specific learning characteristics of the offenders.[37]

The research on recidivism suggests that ex-offenders might be best served engaging in reentry services during their first year after release since that is when they are the most likely to recidivate.

# FEDERAL OFFENDER REENTRY PROGRAMS

Following is a brief description of the main federal programs that have been used to help state and local entities fund activities relating to the reintegration of ex-offenders into local communities. Some of these programs may no longer be receiving funding; these programs are identified below. Other programs that are currently funded may not provide funding for offender reentry purposes every fiscal year. Nevertheless, these programs have been included to provide a comprehensive look at the universe of federal resources that could be used for offender reentry purposes.

## Offender Reentry Programs at the Department of Justice (DOJ)

The first reentry-specific program at the DOJ was the Serious and Violent Offender Reentry Initiative (SVORI), which was coordinated by the Office of Justice Programs (OJP). The SVORI was a federal offender reentry pilot program for adult offenders that focused on coordinating the way federal agencies distribute offender reentry funding. The main federal agencies involved were the Departments of Justice, Labor, Education, and Housing and Urban Development. As part of SVORI, their objective was to help state and local agencies navigate the wide array of existing state formula and block grants and to assist the states and communities to leverage those resources to create comprehensive offender reentry programs. The program distributed $110 million to 69 grantees and concluded in FY2005.

An evaluation of SVORI programs was released in December 2009.[38] The evaluation, among other things, evaluated the post-release outcomes of participants in 16 programs (12 adult and 4 juvenile) in 14 states.[39] The evaluation found that there was little difference in the reported reentry programming needs between offenders who participated in SVORI programs and those who did not participate. Inmates who participated in SVORI programs were more likely to receive reentry programming and services than those who did not participate, but not all SVORI program participants received programming or services. The researchers also found that the provision of services for program participants was below the expressed need for services. Moreover, the provision of services decreased after the inmates were released from confinement. The researchers found that adults who participated in the SVORI program were moderately more likely than non-participants to find housing and employment, not use drugs, and self-report less criminal behavior. However, improvement on these measures (i.e., housing, employment, drug use, and criminal behavior) did not translate into lower levels of reincarceration. Juvenile males who participated in SVORI programs were more likely than non-participants to have a job with benefits 15 months after being released, but there was no significant difference between program participants and non-participants in terms of substance abuse, physical health, mental health, or recidivism.

The Prisoner Reentry Initiative (PRI) was the successor to the SVORI program. According to OJP, the PRI provided funding for model offender reentry programs that focused on providing services and assistance during the three phases of offender reentry: at detention facilities, just prior to and after the offender's release, and during an ex-offender's long-term transition to the community. Congress discontinued funding the PRI after FY2008.

From FY2001 to FY2003, Congress appropriated funding for the DOJ portion of the SVORI under the Community Oriented Policing Services account in the annual Commerce, Justice, Science, and Related Agencies appropriations act. Appropriations were provided during these fiscal years even though they were not authorized. As a part of the 21st Century Department of Justice Reauthorization Act of 2002 (P.L. 107-273), Congress authorized appropriations for an adult and juvenile offender reentry demonstration program. The act originally authorized appropriations of $15.0 million for FY2003, $15.5 million for FY2004, and $16.0 million for FY2005. For FY2004 to FY2008, Congress appropriated funding for the SVORI and the PRI pursuant to the authorization for the adult and juvenile offender reentry demonstration program.

The Second Chance Act of 2007 (P.L. 110-199)[40] reauthorized and modified the scope of the adult and juvenile offender reentry demonstration program. The act replaced the previous four purpose areas eligible for funding with new purpose areas spanning every phase of the offender reentry process. Applicants for these grants are subject to a number of requirements, including submitting a reentry strategic plan with their application, describing the long-term strategy, and providing a detailed implementation schedule, among other things. The act requires that states and localities match 50% of the federal funds provided; up to half of this state match (or 25% of the overall total funding) can be composed of in-kind contributions. The act also created some new demonstration grant programs, including

- grants for state and local reentry courts;
- grants for drug treatment diversion programs;
- grants to expand substance-abuse programs for prisoners and ex-offenders; and
- grants to expand the use of career training programs and mentoring programs.

Since FY2009, funding DOJ for reentry programs has been appropriated pursuant to the grant programs authorized by the Second Chance Act.

## Offender Reentry Programs at Other Federal Agencies

As previously mentioned, many federal departments provide funding through a wide array of programs and block grants, which can be used by states for offender reentry. The following list is not meant to be an exhaustive one, but it does capture many programs run by other departments that can be used to support state offender reentry initiatives.

### *The Department of Labor (DOL)*

The Workforce Investment Act[41] (WIA) of 1998 (P.L. 105-220) authorized a nationwide system of workforce development programs, America's Workforce Network, that provides information and services to connect youths and adults with employers.[42] These programs, which can be used by ex-offenders, provide services such as skills-training and job-placement. DOL also instituted a Young Offender Reentry Demonstration Grant Program, which provides funds to communities for offender reentry programs for offenders aged 14 to 21 who are already in the criminal justice system or are considered high-risk. This program focuses on job-training, education, substance-abuse treatment, mental health care, housing assistance, and family support services.

In addition, DOL maintains two programs that provide incentives for companies to hire ex-offenders. The Work Opportunity Tax Credits program[43] provides up to $2,400 in tax credits to companies for every former offender they hire,[44] and the Federal Bonding Program allows companies who cannot obtain bonding or insurance from their own providers to bond ex-offenders for up to $25,000 for up to six months.[45]

***The Department of Education (DOE)***

The DOE offers programs that can be used by states to help fund or provide technical support for offender reentry programs that focus on education. The Office of Vocational and Adult Education, through the Adult Education and Family Literacy Act (Title II of the Workforce Innovation and Opportunity Act), provides grants to states to support basic education for out-of-school adults. States may allocate up to 20% of their grants to educational services for criminal offenders, including post-release services with the goal of reducing recidivism. In addition, the Perkins State Grant Program allows states to use up to 1% of their funds to serve offenders in institutions.[46]

***The Department of Housing and Urban Development (HUD)***

HUD funds a variety of programs that help states and local governments to support housing programs. The Community Development Block Grant Program aims to assist states in developing viable urban communities. Funds are allocated by formula to the states, and communities and grantees have significant discretion concerning how to allocate their federal funding—including using some funds to provide housing for ex-offenders.[47]

***The Department of Health and Human Services (HHS)***

HHS provides funding for a multitude of programs that can be used to help offender reentry programs through the Substance Abuse and Mental Health Services Agency[48] (SAMHSA) and the Office of Community Services. These programs include the Recovery Community Support Program, which targets people and families recovering from drug abuse and addiction, and several block grant programs. SAMHSA also funds a program that specifically targets offender reentry known as the Young Offender Reentry Program (YORP). The YORP provides funding for state, tribal, and local governments, as well as community based nonprofit organizations, to expand substance abuse treatment and supervision programs for juvenile and young adult offenders re-entering the community.[49] Funds for DHHS programs may be used to provide substance abuse or mental health services for offenders on parole or probation. However, DHHS funds may not be used to provide services to incarcerated offenders.[50]

## Coordination Between Federal Agencies

A number of entities bring together offender reentry professionals from state and local governments, nonprofit organizations, and academic institutions, including the Reentry Policy Council founded by the Council of State Governments and the Reentry Roundtable hosted by the Urban Institute. Both of these organizations attempt to bolster information sharing about best practices and funding opportunities and coordination between the various state and local agencies and stake-holders within the offender reentry field.

The DOJ has started an interagency Reentry Council to coordinate federal reentry efforts and advance effective reentry policies. The purpose of the council is "to bring together numerous federal agencies to make communities safer, assist those returning from prison and jail in becoming productive, tax-paying citizens, and save taxpayer dollars by lowering the direct and collateral costs of incarceration."[51] The council includes representatives from the following agencies and offices:

- Department of Justice,
- Department of the Interior,
- Department of Agriculture,
- Department of Labor,
- Department of Health and Human Services,
- Department of Housing and Urban Development,
- Department of Education,
- Department of Veterans Affairs,
- Office of National Drug Control Policy,
- Social Security Administration,
- Domestic Policy Council,
- Equal Employment Opportunity Commission,
- White House Office of Faith-Based and Neighborhood Partnerships,
- Office of Personnel Management,
- Office of Management and Budget,
- Internal Revenue Service,
- Federal Trade Commission,

- Interagency Council on Homelessness, and
- Small Business Administration.

## CONCLUSION

Over the past two and a half decades, the prison population and the number of ex-offenders being released into the community have been increasing. The increasing number of ex-offenders entering the community has put pressure on public policy makers to provide treatments and services that will smooth the reintegration process while reducing recidivism. When deciding what programs to fund, policy makers often focus on reducing recidivism. The focus on reducing recidivism, however, is complicated by the fact that there are different definitions of recidivism. For example, the most recent major national-level study showed that within five years of their release three-quarters of ex-offenders came into contact with the legal system and about half were back in prison for either a new conviction or a violation of the terms of their release. However, only a quarter of the ex-offenders ended up in prison for having committed new crimes. Whether technical violations should be considered a measure of recidivism or whether recidivism should be confined to the commission of new crimes has engendered much debate within the criminal justice field.

While the emphasis on reducing recidivism is important, programs can also be evaluated based on other outcome measures such as their ability to connect ex-offenders with jobs, services, and institutions in their communities. The best available research has shown that there are a number of services that can help ex-offenders reconnect with their communities and lower recidivism, including programs focusing on providing vocational training, substance abuse prevention, mental health services, and housing. The reportedly most successful programs focus on high-risk offenders, are intensive in nature, begin during institutional placement, and take place mostly in the community. However, a relative lack of scientifically rigorous research has made it difficult to draw definitive conclusions about which programs are most effective.

As Congress considers this issue, a number of policy issues may be assessed, including whether the current federal grant programs are adequate or whether new programs should be created, whether there is a need for more regular national-level recidivism data (there were almost 20 years between the BJS's two reports on recidivism), whether enough coordination of the many programs that may be used to help ex-offenders is occurring within the federal government, whether more evaluations of offender reentry programs are needed, and whether funding will be appropriated for the programs and activities that were authorized by the Second Chance Act.

# APPENDIX A. SECTION-BY-SECTION SUMMARY OF THE SECOND CHANCE ACT

The Second Chance Act, P.L. 110-199, was passed by the House on November 13, 2007, and by the Senate on March 11, 2008. The act was signed into law on April 9, 2008. Following is a section-by-section summary of the act's provisions.

## Amendments to Current Offender Reentry Grant Program (§101)

The Second Chance Act reauthorized and expanded the adult and juvenile offender state and local offender reentry demonstration projects codified at 42 U.S.C. §3797w. The act amended the prior authorization for the program so than grant funds can be used within seven broad purpose areas:

- educational, literacy, vocational, and job placement services;
- substance abuse treatment and services, including programs that start in placement and continue through the community;
- programs that provide comprehensive supervision and offer services in the community, including programs that provide housing assistance and mental and physical health services;
- programs that focus on family integration during and after placement for both offenders and their families;
- mentoring programs that start in placement and continue into the community;
- programs that provide victim-appropriate services, including those that promote the timely payment of restitution by offenders and those that offer services (such as security or counseling) to victims when offenders are released; and

- programs that protect communities from dangerous offenders, including developing and implementing the use of risk assessment tools to determine when offenders should be released from prison.

Applicants for these grants are subjected to a number of requirements, including submitting a reentry strategic plan with their application, describing the long-term strategy, providing a detailed implementation schedule, identifying the local government's role in the plan, and describing the "evidence based methodology and outcome measures" that are used to evaluate the programs and "provide valid measures" of the program's impact.

The act allows the Attorney General (AG) to make grants for these programs if the applications received meet the following conditions:

- they are explicitly supported by the chief executive of the unit of government applying for the funding;
- they extensively discuss the role that the various law enforcement entities involved in the reentry process will have in the program;
- they provide extensive evidence of collaboration among the state and local health, housing, child welfare, education, substance abuse, victims services, employment, and law enforcement agencies;
- they provide a plan for analyzing any statutory, regulatory, or other hurdles that may exist to reintegrating offenders into the community; and
- they include a reentry taskforce as described below to carry out the activities funded under the grant.

The act requires applicants to develop a comprehensive strategic reentry plan that contains measurable five-year performance outcomes, with the goal of reducing recidivism by 50% over this period. As a condition of funding, applicants are also required to create offender reentry taskforces that integrate the prime offender reentry stake-holders in their communities in order to pool resources, facilitate data-collection, and reduce recidivism. Grantees are also required to submit annual reports to DOJ that identify the specific progress made toward achieving their strategic performance outcomes, and may be eligible for future grants if they demonstrate adequate progress towards reducing recidivism by 10% over a two-year period.

In awarding grants under this program, the AG is directed to prioritize applications that

- focus on geographic areas with a disproportionate population of ex-offenders;
- include input from nonprofit organizations, consultation with victims and ex-offenders, and coordinate with families;
- demonstrate effective case management in order to provide comprehensive and continuous services during reentry;
- review the adjudications process for parole violations in the applicant's criminal justice system;
- provide for an independent evaluation of the program, including, to the extent practicable, the use of random assignment; and
- target high risk offenders through the use of validated assessment tools.

Additionally, the act established a National Adult and Juvenile Offender Reentry Resource Center by authorizing the AG to make a grant available to an eligible organization. The selected organization is directed to provide education, training, and technical assistance to states and other governments in order to collect and disseminate data and best practices in offender reentry, including the use of evaluation tools and other measures to assess and document performance. Up to 4% of the authorized level of funding can be used to establish and run this center.

The act authorized $55 million in both FY2009 and FY2010 for these programs and limits funding for technical assistance and training to between 2% and 3% of the overall total appropriated. The total federal share of funding for these grants is limited to 50%; however, up to 50% of the state and local matching funds (i.e., 25% of the overall grant) can be fulfilled through in-kind contributions of goods or services.

## Improvement of the Residential Substance Abuse Treatment for State Offenders Program (§102)

This provision requires states receiving grants under the residential substance abuse treatment program (42 U.S.C. 3796ff) to ensure that individuals participating in these programs receive aftercare services, including a full continuum of support services. The act defines residential substance abuse treatment programs as a course of comprehensive individual and group substance abuse services lasting at least six months in residential treatment facilities that are set apart from the general population of a prison or jail. The act also requires the AG to study the use and effectiveness of the funds used to provide the required aftercare services.

## Definition of Violent Offender for Drug Court Program (§103)

The act modified the government's current drug court grant program, restricting the current definition of "violent offender" to individuals charged with or convicted for certain offenses that are punishable by a sentence of longer than one year (prior there was no minimum sentence length).[52] The act requires all grantees under this program to adhere to this definition of "violent offender" within three years of the enactment of the act (i.e., April 9, 2011).

## New Offender Reentry Grant Programs

Subtitle B created a number of new targeted grant programs within the Department of Justice (DOJ) relating to the reintegration of offenders into the community.

## State and Local Reentry Courts (§111)

This provision created a new grant program within DOJ to fund reentry courts. Subject to the availability of appropriations, grants up to $500,000 are made available for state and local adult and juvenile court systems in order to establish and maintain reentry courts. These courts are tasked with monitoring juvenile and adult offenders reentering into the community and providing them with a coordinated and comprehensive array of services, including housing assistance, education, job training, health services, and substance abuse treatment. In order to be eligible for funding, applicants have to demonstrate the need for their program; create a long-term strategy and detailed implementation plan; identify the government and community entities that would be coordinated by the project; and describe the methodology and outcome measures that would be used to evaluate the program. Additionally, applicants are required to submit annual reports to DOJ including a summary of the activities carried out with the grant and an assessment of whether these activities are meeting the needs identified in the grant application. The act authorized $10 million for this program in FY2009 and FY2010. The total federal share of funding for these grants is limited to 50%; however, up to 50% of the state and local matching funds (i.e., 25% of the overall grant) could be fulfilled through in-kind contributions of goods or services.

## Drug Treatment Alternative to Prison Programs (§112)

This provision created a new grant program for state and local prosecutors to fund the development, implementation, and expansion of drug treatment programs that are alternatives to imprisonment. The programs require eligible offenders, after having received the consent of the prosecutor, to participate in comprehensive drug treatment programs in lieu of imprisonment. Criminal charges would be dismissed upon completion of the program. Offenders failing to successfully complete their treatment programs would serve their original sentence. In order to be eligible for these programs, the offender in question could not have had any prior felony use of force convictions or have been charged with or convicted of an offense involving a firearm, a dangerous weapon, or the use of force against another individual. The act authorized $10 million for this program in FY2009 and FY2010. The total federal share of funding for these grants is limited to 50%; however, up to 50% of the state and local matching funds (i.e., 25% of the overall grant) could be fulfilled through in-kind contributions of goods or services.

## Family Substance Abuse Treatment Alternatives to Incarceration Grants (§113)

This provision created a new grant program to develop, implement, and expand the use of family-based substance abuse treatment programs as alternatives to incarceration for non-violent parent drug offenders. Among other things, the treatment is required to be clinically appropriate, comprehensive, and long-term and would be provided in a residential setting rather than an outpatient or a hospital setting. The program is required to include the implementation of graduated sanctions applied on the basis of the offender's accountability throughout the course of the program and the development of reentry plans for offenders. Offenders failing to complete the program are required to complete the sentence for the underlying crime involved. Grantees are required to submit annual reports to DOJ detailing the effectiveness of their programs using evidence-based data. Prison-based programs are required to locate their programs in an area separate from the general population, to create and support treatment plans for incarcerated parents, and to ensure continuity of care if participating offenders are transferred to a different facility. The act authorized $10 million in FY2009 and in FY2010 for these grants; not less than 5% of this total is to be allocated to Indian tribes.

## Grants to Evaluate and Improve Educational Methods at Prisons, Jails, and Juvenile Facilities (§114)

This program authorizes the AG, subject to the availability of appropriations, to make grants to evaluate, identify, and improve programs that focus on providing educational and vocational programs for offenders by identifying and implementing best practices. Grantees are required to submit reports within 90 days of the last day of the final fiscal year of a grant detailing the progress that they have made. The act authorized appropriations of $5 million for this program for FY2009 and FY2010.

## Technology Careers Training Demonstration Grants (§115)

The act authorizes the AG to make grants to states, units of local governments, territories, and Indian Tribes to provide technology career training for prisoners. Grants may be awarded for programs that establish technology careers training programs for offenders during the three-year period prior to their release. Access to the Internet during the program is restricted to ensure public safety. Grantees must submit a report to DOJ describing and assessing the program each fiscal year. The act authorized $10 million for this program in FY2009 and FY2010.

## New Drug-Treatment and Mentoring Grant Programs

Title II of P.L. 110-199 authorized a series of new grant programs for drug-treatment and mentoring purposes. Subtitle A (§201) focuses on drug treatment programs, Subtitles B and C (§§211-214) focus on training and mentoring programs, and Subtitle C (§231) created a federal offender reentry program at the Bureau of Prisons.

## Offender Reentry Substance Abuse and Criminal Justice Collaboration Program (§201)

The act authorized the AG to make grants to states, units of local governments, territories, and Indian tribes in order to improve drug treatment programs in prisons and reduce the use of alcohol and other drugs by long-term abusers under correctional supervision. Grants may be used to continue or improve existing drug treatment programs, develop and implement programs for long-term substance abusers, provide addiction recovery support services, and establish pharmacological drug treatment services as part of any drug treatment program offered to prisoners.[53] Grant applicants are required to identify the entities that will be involved in providing the treatment, certify that this treatment has been developed in consultation with the Single State Authority for Substance Abuse,[54] certify that the treatment will be clinically appropriate and will provide comprehensive treatment, and describe how evidence-based strategies have been incorporated into the program, including the collection and analysis of data. The AG was required to submit a report to Congress detailing best practices relating to substance abuse treatment in prison and comprehensive treatment of long-term substance abusers by September 30, 2009. Another report on the drug treatment programs funded through this grant program was required by September 30, 2010. The act authorized appropriations of $15 million for this program for both FY2009 and FY2010.

## Mentoring Grants to Nonprofit Organizations (§211)

This provision created a new grant program to provide mentoring and other transitional services for offenders being released into the community. Funding can be used for mentoring programs both in placement and during reentry, programs providing transition services during reentry, and programs providing training for "offender and victims issues." Priority is given to applicants providing for the evaluation of their programs, using randomized control trials to the maximum extent feasible. Applicants are required to identify and report on specific outcome performance measures related to the overall goal of reducing recidivism. The act authorized $15 million in FY2009 and in FY2010 for these grants.

## Responsible Reintegration of Offenders (§212)

The act authorized the Secretary of Labor to make grants to nonprofit organizations to provide a wide array of mentoring, job training and job placement services, and other comprehensive transitional services. Grants may not be used to provide substance abuse treatment, mental health treatment, or housing services; however, grants can be used to coordinate with other entities providing these services. Applications for the program must identify the specific eligible area that will be served and the need for support in this area and describe the services that will be provided, the partnerships that have been established with the criminal justice system and housing authorities, and how other sources of funding will be leveraged to provide support services. In order to be eligible for funding, programs must be located in urbanized areas or clusters (as determined by the Bureau of the Census) that have a large number of prisoners returning to the community and high recidivism rates (however, no definitions for a large number of returning prisoners or high recidivism rates are provided). To be eligible for the program, offenders must be at least 18 years old, have no prior adult convictions or convictions for violent or sex-related offenses, and have been released from prison no more than 180 days before they begin participating in the grant program.[55] The act authorized $20 million in appropriations for the Secretary of Labor to carry out this section in both FY2009 and FY2010; up to 4% of the appropriation may be used to provide technical assistance.

## Bureau of Prisons Policies on Mentoring Contacts (§213)

This provision directed the Director of the Bureau of Prisons (BOP) to adopt and implement a policy by July 9, 2009, to ensure that mentors working with incarcerated offenders are permitted to continue providing their services to the offender after their release from prison. The Director was required to submit a report to Congress concerning this policy's implementation by September 20, 2009.

## Bureau of Prisons Policies on Chapel Library Material (§214)

The Director of the BOP was required to discontinue the Standardized Chapel Library project, or any other project that compiles, lists, or restricts prisoner access to materials provided by chapel libraries by May 9, 2008. Exceptions were made for materials that incite, promote, or suggest violence and materials prohibited by law.

## Federal Prisoner Reentry Program (§231)

The act establishes a prisoner reentry program within the BOP. BOP was required to create a federal prisoner reentry strategy that

- assesses each prisoner's skill level at the beginning of their prison term (including academic, vocational, health, cognitive, interpersonal, daily living, and other related skills);
- creates a skills development plan for prisoners to be carried out during their term of imprisonment;
- determines program assignments for prisoners based on the needs identified by the assessment;
- gives priority to the reentry needs of high-risk populations, including sex-offenders, career criminals, and prisoners with mental health problems;
- coordinates and collaborates with other criminal justice, community-based, and faith-based organizations;
- collects information about a prisoner's family relationships and parental responsibilities; and
- provides incentives for prisoners to participate in skills development programs.

Incentives for prisoners to participate in skills development programs include allowing offenders to spend the maximum amount of time in community confinement facilities. Additionally, BOP was required to assist offenders in obtaining identification prior to their release.

The act modified current law to include a number of new duties for the Director of BOP. These new duties include the establishment of prerelease planning procedures for all federal offenders that help prisoners apply for federal and state benefits prior to their release, and the establishment of reentry planning procedures to provide federal offenders with information in a number of reentry-related areas. The BOP was required to establish and implement a system that will allow it to quantitatively track progress in responding to the reentry needs of its inmates and to provide an annual report to the House and Senate Committees on the Judiciary concerning its progress. An annual report is also required containing recidivism statistics for federal prisoners, including information concerning the relative recidivism rates of offenders participating in major inmate programs. After the initial report establishes a baseline recidivism rate for BOP ex-offenders, the act established 5- and 10-year goals of 2% and 5% reductions in this rate, respectively.

The BOP was further required to ensure that the United States Probation and Pretrial Services System has medical information for inmates scheduled for release in order to create supervision plans that address the medical and mental health care needs of ex-offenders, and to ensure that each prisoner in community confinement has access to medical and mental health care.

In addition to the offender reentry program established above, the act also established two new programs within the BOP:

- A pilot program within the BOP to determine the effectiveness of allowing certain elderly, non-violent offenders to serve the remainder of their sentences on home detention. In order to be eligible for this program, offenders have to be 65 years old or older and have never been convicted of a violent or sex-related crime or given a life-sentence, among other things.
- A program to provide satellite tracking of certain high-risk individuals after their release from prison, in conjunction with the use of graduated sanctions, the provision of reentry related services, and the involvement the offender's family, a victim advocate, and the victim. The act authorized $5 million for this purpose for FY2009 and in FY2010.

## Authorization of Appropriations for Research (§245)

The act authorized $10 million in both FY2009 and FY2010 to carry out the research programs authorized by §§241-244.

## Clarification of Authority to Place Prisoner in Community Corrections (§251)

This provision required the Director of the BOP to ensure, to the extent practicable, that prisoners within the federal correctional system spend up to a year at the end of their sentence focusing on their reentry into the community. As part of this practice, the BOP is authorized to transfer offenders to community correctional facilities or to home confinement (for the shorter of the last 10% or six months of their sentence). The provision also gives BOP the discretion to disregard a court's order that an offender serve part of his sentence in a community correctional facility.

## Residential Drug Abuse Program in Federal Prisons (§252)

The act replaced the current definition of a residential drug abuse program with language defining such a program as a course of individual and group activities and treatment lasting at least six months in residential treatment facilities that are set apart from the general prison population. The act also stipulated that this treatment can include pharmacotherapies that extend beyond the six-month period.

## Contracting for Services for Post-Conviction Supervision of Offenders (§253)

This provision gives the Director of the Administrative Office of the United States Courts the authority to enter into contracts with public and private agencies to monitor and provide a wide array of services to offenders in the community to promote their reintegration.

## Extension of National Prison Rape Elimination Commission (§261)

The act extended the authorization for the National Prison Rape Elimination Commission[56] from three years to five years.

# Appendix B. Appropriations for DOJ Reentry Grant Programs

### Table B-1.Authorized and Appropriated Funding for the DOJ Reentry Program, FY2001-FY2008

Appropriations and authorizations in millions of dollars

| Fiscal Year | Authorized | Appropriated |
|---|---|---|
| 2001 | N.A. | $29.9 |
| 2002 | N.A. | 14.9 |
| 2003 | 15.0 | 14.8 |
| 2004 | 15.5 | 4.9 |
| 2005 | 16.0 | 9.9 |
| 2006 | N.A. | 4.9 |
| 2007 | N.A. | 14.9 |
| 2008 | N.A. | 11.8 |

Source: Data provided by the U.S. Department of Justice, Community Oriented Policing Services Office.

Notes: "N.A." means "not authorized." Starting with FY2009, Congress started appropriating funding for DOJ's reentry program pursuant to the Second Chance Act (see Table B-2). Appropriated amount includes all rescissions of current year budget authority.

### Table B-2. Authorized and Appropriated Funding for the Second Chance Act Grant Programs Administered by the Department of Justice, FY2009-FY2015

Appropriations and authorizations in millions of dollars

| Fiscal Year | Authorized | Appropriated |
|---|---|---|
| 2009 | $160.0 | $25.0[a] |
| 2010 | 160.0 | 100.0[b] |
| 2011 | N.A. | 82.8[c] |
| 2012 | N.A. | 63.0[d] |
| 2013 | N.A. | 63.9[e] |
| 2014 | N.A. | 67.8[f] |
| 2015 | N.A. | 68.0[g] |

Source: FY2009 appropriations were taken from P.L. 111-8; FY2010 appropriations were taken from P.L. 111- 117; FY2011 appropriations were based on a CRS analysis of the text of P.L. 112-10; FY2012 appropriation was taken from P.L. 112-55; FY2013 appropriation was provided by the Department of Justice;

FY2014 appropriation was taken from the joint explanatory statement to accompany P.L. 113-76, printed in the January 15, 2014, Congressional Record (pp. H507-H532); FY2015 appropriation was taken from the joint explanatory statement to accompany P.L. 113-235, printed in the December 12, 2014, Congressional Record (pp. H9342-H9363).

Notes: "N.A." means "not authorized." Appropriated amount includes all rescissions of current year budget authority.

[a] The FY2009 appropriation included $15 million for the Adult and Juvenile Offender Reentry Demonstration program and $10 million for mentoring grants to nonprofit organizations.

[b] The FY2010 appropriation included $37 million for the Adult and Juvenile Offender Reentry Demonstration program; $10 million for state and local reentry courts; $7.5 million for Family Substance Abuse Treatment Alternative to Incarceration grants; $2.5 million for grants to evaluate and improve education methods at prisons, jails, and juvenile facilities; $5 million for Technology Careers Training Demonstration grants; $13 million for the Offender Reentry Substance Abuse and Criminal Justice Collaboration program; $15 million for Mentoring Grants to Nonprofit Organizations; and $10 million for grants for offender reentry research.

[c] The FY2011 appropriation included $30.6 million for the Adult and Juvenile Offender Reentry Demonstration program; $8.3 million for state and local reentry courts; $6.2 million for Family Substance Abuse Treatment Alternative to Incarceration grants; $2.1 million for grants to evaluate and improve education methods at prisons, jails, and juvenile facilities; $4.1 million for Technology Careers Training Demonstration grants; $10.8 million for the Offender Reentry Substance Abuse and Criminal Justice Collaboration program; $12.4 million for Mentoring Grants to Nonprofit Organizations; and $8.3 million for grants for offender reentry research.

[d] For FY2012, $63 million was provided for DOJ-administered grant programs authorized under the Second Chance Act, of which $4 million was set aside for a smart probation program. Congress allowed the Administration to decide how the remaining $59 million would be allocated between the programs authorized under the act.

[e] For FY2013, $63.9 million was provided for DOJ-administered grant programs authorized under the Second Chance Act, of which $4.6 million was set aside for a smart probation program. Congress allowed the Administration to decide how the remaining $63.8 million would be allocated between the programs authorized under the act. The FY2013 enacted amount also includes the amount sequestered per the Budget Control Act of 2011(P.L. 112-25).

[f] For FY2014, $67.8 million was provided for DOJ-administered grant programs authorized under the Second Chance Act, of which $6 million was set aside for a smart probation program, $2 million was set aside for a Children of Incarcerated Parents Demonstration Grant program, and $7.5 million was set aside for a "Pay for Success" program. Congress allowed the Administration to decide how the

remaining $52.3 million would be allocated between the programs authorized under the act.

[g] For FY2015, $68.0 million was provided for DOJ-administered grant programs authorized under the Second Chance Act, of which $6 million was set aside for a smart probation program, $5 million was set aside for a Children of Incarcerated Parents Demonstration Grant program, and $7.5 million was set aside for a "Pay for Success" program. Congress allowed the Administration to decide how the remaining $49.5 million would be allocated between the programs authorized under the act.

## End Notes

[1] U.S. Department of Justice, Office of Justice Programs, Bureau of Justice Statistics, "Reentry Trends in the United States," http://www.bjs.gov/content/reentry/reentry.cfm; hereinafter "Reentry Trends."

[2] E. Ann Carson and Daniela Golinelli, Prisoners in 2012: Trends in Admissions and Releases 1991-2012, U.S. Department of Justice, Office of Justice Programs, Bureau of Justice Statistics, NCJ 243920, Washington, DC, December 2013, p. 3.

[3] Matthew R. Durose, Alexia D. Cooper, and Howard N. Snyder, Recidivism of Prisoners Released in 30 States in 2005: Patterns from 2005 to 2010, NCJ 244205, April 2014, p. 1.

[4] Wilkinson, Reginald A., Director of the Ohio Department of Rehabilitation and Correction, "Offender Reentry: A Storm Overdue," Paper Prepared for Third National Forum on Restorative Justice, March 2002, on file with the author. Hereinafter "A Storm Overdue."

[5] Tracey Kyckelhahn, State Corrections Expenditures, FY1982-2010, U.S. Department of Justice, Office of Justice Programs, Bureau of Justice Statistics, NCJ239672, Washington, DC, December 2012, p. 4, http://www.bjs.gov/ content/pub/pdf/scefy8210.pdf.

[6] Ibid., p. 11.

[7] U.S. Department of Justice, Office of Justice Programs, "Learn About Reentry," http://www.reentry.gov/learn.html.

[8] While this is generally the case, jails on occasion can also include individuals sentenced to prison terms lasting less than one year (misdemeanors) and convicted felons in jurisdictions where the prisons are overpopulated.

[9] Reentry Trends.

[10] A determinate sentence is a fixed sentence, while an indeterminate sentence is typically expressed as a range (i.e., 5 to 10 years).

[11] For an expanded discussion of the varying definitions of recidivism, refer to Allen Beck, Recidivism: A Fruit Salad Concept in the Criminal Justice World, Justice Concepts, available at http://www.justiceconcepts.com/recidivism.pdf.

[12] The 1994 BJS study examined the rearrest, reconviction, and reincarceration of prisoners from 15 states three years after their release in 1994. The study tracked 272,111 prisoners, or almost two-thirds of all the prisoners released from state prisons in 1994. Patrick A. Langan and David J. Levin, Recidivism of Prisoners Released in 1994, NCJ193427, June 2002.

[13] Matthew R. Durose, Alexia D. Cooper, and Howard N. Snyder, Recidivism of Prisoners Released in 30 States in 2005: Patterns from 2005 to 2010, NCJ 244205, April 2014.

[14] The BJS cautions that because of factors like the different attributes of the prisoners included in the 1994 and 2005 study, better data on inmates released in 2005 who died during the follow-up period, and improvements in the completeness of criminal history records, the results of the 2005 study are not directly comparable to the results of the 1994 study. Ibid., pp. 2-5.

[15] "Adjudicated" refers to arrests that resulted in a subsequent court adjudication or disposition (e.g., convictions, dismissals, acquittals, or deferred adjudications).

[16] "Returned to prison" refers to arrests that resulted in a conviction with a disposition of a prison sentence or when prisoners were returned to prison without a new conviction due to technical violations of the terms of their release (e.g., failing a drug test or missing an appointment with a parole officer).

[17] "Incarcerated" refers to arrests that resulted in a prison or jail sentence.

[18] "Imprisoned" refers to arrests that resulted in a prison sentence.

[19] Richard P. Seiter and Karen R. Kadela, "Prisoner Reentry: What Works, What Does Not, and What Is Promising," Crime & Delinquency, vol. 49, no. 3, 2003, pp. 360-388; hereinafter "Prisoner Reentry: What Works."

[20] Questioning the Evidence, 4-5.

[21] Questioning the Evidence, p. 5.

[22] Prisoner Reentry: What Works, p. 370.

[23] Meta-analyses are a type of systematic review of studies that allow researchers to draw conclusions across a wide range of studies by using statistical methods to derive quantitative results from the analysis of multiple sources of quantitative evidence.

[24] Lawrence W. Sherman, Denise Gottfredson, Doris MacKenzie, John Eck, Peter Reuter, and Shawn Bushway, Preventing Crime: What Works, What Doesn't, What's Promising, National Institute of Justice, 1997.

[25] Prisoner Reentry: What Works.

[26] Prisoner Reentry: What Works, pp. 370-373.

[27] The Council of State Governments, Justice Center, National Reentry Resource Center, What Works in Reentry Clearinghouse, http://whatworks.csgjusticecenter.org/.

[28] The Council of State Governments, Justice Center, National Reentry Resource Center, What Works in Reentry Clearinghouse: Employment, http://whatworks.csgjusticecenter.org/focus_areas/employment-topic.

[29] The Council of State Governments, Justice Center, National Reentry Resource Center, What Works in Reentry Clearinghouse: Substance Abuse, http://whatworks.csgjusticecenter.org/focus_areas/substance-abuse.

[30] Therapeutic communities offer an environment in which participants receive treatment and other services in a housing area separated from the rest of the incarcerated population.

[31] The Council of State Governments, Justice Center, National Reentry Resource Center, What Works in Reentry Clearinghouse: Education, http://whatworks.csgjusticecenter.org/focus_areas/education.

[32] There was one study that evaluated an ABE program, two that evaluated GED programs, and another two the evaluated post-secondary education programs.

[33] The Council of State Governments, Justice Center, National Reentry Resource Center, What Works in Reentry Clearinghouse: Mental Health, http://whatworks.csgjusticecenter.org/focus_areas/mental-health.

[34] Generally speaking, programs that use a continuity of care approach provide intensive case management while the prisoner is incarcerated, refer him or her to outside service providers

prior to release, and continue to offer post-release case management and other services in the community.

[35] The Council of State Governments, Justice Center, National Reentry Resource Center, What Works in Reentry Clearinghouse: Housing, http://whatworks.csgjusticecenter.org/focus_areas/housing.

[36] Ibid.

[37] Questioning the Evidence, pp. 6-7.

[38] Pamela K. Lattimore and Christy A. Visher, The Multi-site Evaluation of SVORI: Summary and Synthesis, RTI International, December 2009, https://www.ncjrs.gov/pdffiles1/nij/grants/230421.pdf.

[39] The evaluation included a pre-release interview (conducted approximately 30 day before being released) with both SVORI and non-SVORI participants. Follow-up interviews were conducted 3, 9, and 15 months after release. In addition, oral swab drug tests were conducted during the 3 and 15 month interviews. Recidivism data was collected from the Federal Bureau of Investigation's National Crime Information Center (NCIC) and state correctional and juvenile justice agencies. Ibid., p. ES-7.

[40] A more detailed description of the Second Chance Act can be found in the Appendix A.

[41] U.S. Department of Labor, Employment & Training Administration, "Serious and Violent Offender Reentry Initiative Appendices," http://www.doleta.gov/grants/sga/ reentry_app.cfm; hereinafter "Serious and Violent Offender Reentry Initiative Appendices."

[42] For more information about the Workforce Investment Act, please refer to CRS Report RL33687, The Workforce Investment Act (WIA): Program-by-Program Overview and Funding of Title I Training Programs, by David H. Bradley.

[43] For more information about the Work Opportunity Tax Credits Program, please refer to CRS Report R43729, The Work Opportunity Tax Credit, by Benjamin Collins and Sarah A. Donovan.

[44] U.S. Department of Labor, Employment & Training Administration, "Work Opportunity Tax Credit" available at http://www.doleta.gov/business/Incentives/opptax/.

[45] U.S. Department of Labor, Employment & Training Administration, "Federal Bonding Program," http://www.bonds4jobs.com/program-background.html.

[46] "Serious and Violent Offender Reentry Initiative Appendices"

[47] Ibid.

[48] For more information about SAMHSA, see CRS Report R41477, Substance Abuse and Mental Health Services Administration (SAMHSA): Agency Overview and Reauthorization Issues, by C. Stephen Redhead.

[49] Testimony of Senior Policy Advisor to the Administrator Cheri Nolan, Substance Abuse and Mental Health Services Administration, U.S. Department of Health and Human Services, before the Committee on the Judiciary, Subcommittee on Corrections and Rehabilitation, Thursday, September 21, 2006.

[50] "Serious and Violent Offender Reentry Initiative Appendices."

[51] National Reentry Resource Center, Federal Interagency Reentry Council, http://csgjusticecenter.org/nrrc/projects/ firc/.

[52] In order to be considered a "violent offender," an individual has to have committed this crime while in possession of a firearm or dangerous weapon, the crime has to have resulted in the death or serious bodily injury of a person, force had to have been used against someone's person, or the offender had 1 or more prior convictions for a felony crime of violence involving the use or attempted use of force against a person with the intent to cause death or serious bodily harm. See 42 U.S.C. §3797 u-2(a)(1).

[53] Pharmacological drug treatment involves using drugs and medications in the treatment of substance abuse. See Clayton Mosher, Scott Akins, and Chad Smith, "Pharmacological Drug Treatment" Paper presented at the annual meeting of the American Society of Criminology, Royal York, Toronto. 2008-04-21.

[54] States would be required to identify an entity that would be the single State administrative authority responsible for planning, developing, implementing, monitoring, regulating, and evaluating substance abuse services within the State.

[55] Grantees may exempt 10% of their clients from this 180-day requirement.

[56] 42 U.S.C. §15606(d)(3)(A).

In: Challenges to the Federal Prison System ... ISBN: 978-1-63484-236-5
Editor: Bryan M. Walker 

*Chapter 3*

# RECIDIVISM OF PRISONERS RELEASED IN 30 STATES IN 2005: PATTERNS FROM 2005 TO 2010*

***Matthew R. Durose, Alexia D. Cooper and Howard N. Snyder***

## HIGHLIGHTS

Among state prisoners released in 30 states in 2005—

- About two-thirds (67.8%) of released prisoners were arrested for a new crime within 3 years, and three-quarters (76.6%) were arrested within 5 years.
- Within 5 years of release, 82.1% of property offenders were arrested for a new crime, compared to 76.9% of drug offenders, 73.6% of public order offenders, and 71.3% of violent offenders.
- More than a third (36.8%) of all prisoners who were arrested within 5 years of release were arrested within the first 6 months after release, with more than half (56.7%) arrested by the end of the first year.

* This is an edited, reformatted and augmented version of a special report, NCJ 244205, issued by the U.S. Department of Justice, Bureau of Justice Statistics, April 2014.

- Two in five (42.3%) released prisoners were either not arrested or arrested once in the 5 years after their release.
- A sixth (16.1%) of released prisoners were responsible for almost half (48.4%) of the nearly 1.2 million arrests that occurred in the 5-year follow-up period.
- An estimated 10.9% of released prisoners were arrested in a state other than the one that released them during the 5-year follow-up period.
- Within 5 years of release, 84.1% of inmates who were age 24 or younger at release were arrested, compared to 78.6% of inmates ages 25 to 39 and 69.2% of those age 40 or older.

Overall, 67.8% of the 404,638 state prisoners released in 2005 in 30 states were arrested within 3 years of release, and 76.6% were arrested within 5 years of release *(figure 1).* Among prisoners released in 2005 in 23 states with available data on inmates returned to prison, 49.7% had either a parole or probation violation or an arrest for a new offense within 3 years that led to imprisonment, and 55.1% had a parole or probation violation or an arrest that led to imprisonment within 5 years.

While prior Bureau of Justice Statistics (BJS) prisoner recidivism reports tracked inmates for 3 years following release, this report used a 5-year follow-up period. The longer window provides supplementary information for policymakers and practitioners on the officially recognized criminal behavior of released prisoners. While 20.5% of released prisoners not arrested within 2 years of release were arrested in the third year, the percentage fell to 13.3% among those who had not been arrested within 4 years. The longer recidivism period also provides a more complete assessment of the number and types of crimes committed by released persons in the years following their release.

## Factors Contributing to Differences with Prior BJS Studies

Policymakers, practitioners, researchers, and the general public may be interested in understanding how the 2005 prisoner recidivism rates in this report compare with those in the previous BJS recidivism study that measured prisoners released in 1994. While both the 1994 and 2005 studies were based on systematic samples of persons released from state prisons, direct comparisons between the published recidivism statistics should not be made.

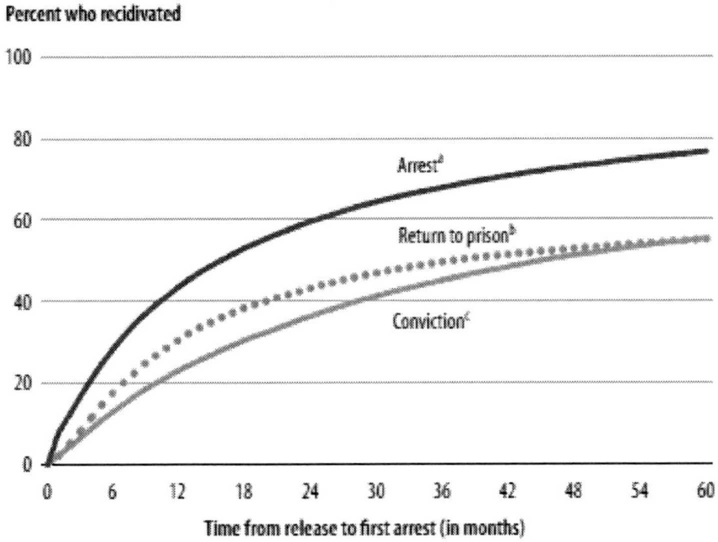


Source: Bureau of Justice Statistics, Recidivism of State Prisoners Released in 2005 data collection.

Note: Prisoners were tracked for 5 years following release in 30 states. Some states were excluded from the specific measures of recidivism. See *Methodology*.

[a] Based on time from release to first arrest among inmates released in 30 states.

[b] Based on time from release to first arrest that led to a prison sentence or first prison admission for a technical violation without a new sentence among inmates released in 23 states. [c]Based on time from release to first arrest that led to a conviction among inmates released in 29 states.

Figure 1. Recidivism of prisoners released in 30 states in 2005, by time from release to first arrest that led to recidivating event.

## Adjustments for Some Differences in the 1994 and 2005 Prison Populations Are Possible

One reason for not directly comparing the 1994 and 2005 recidivism estimates relates to differences in the attributes of the prisoners included in the two samples. The number of states contributing released prisoners to the study increased from 15 in 1994 to 30 in 2005. To control for this difference, BJS conducted analyses that limited the comparison to the post-release arrest rates among the inmates released in the 12 states (California, Florida, Maryland, Michigan, Minnesota, New Jersey, New York, North Carolina, Ohio, Oregon, Texas, and Virginia) that participated in both studies. Among the inmates released in these 12 states, an estimated 66.9% of the 249,657 inmates released in 1994 were arrested for a new crime within 3 years, compared to an estimated 69.3% of the 286,829 inmates released in 2005—a 2.4 percentage point difference.

Another difference between the two studies involved the demographic and offending characteristics of prisoners released from the state prisons, attributes known to be related to recidivism. For example, the proportion of inmates who were age 40 or older at release increased from 17.2% in the 1994 sample to 32.1% in the 2005 sample. In addition, the proportion who were in prison for a violent offense increased from 22.4% in the 1994 sample to 27.4% in the 2005 sample (table 1).

BJS standardized the demographic (i.e., sex, race, Hispanic origin, and age) and commitment offense distribution of the 2005 cohort to the distribution of the 1994 cohort to control for the effects these factors had on the overall recidivism estimates. (See *Methodology* for more information.) These calculations produced the 3-year arrest rate of prisoners released in 2005 that would have been observed if the 2005 release cohort had the characteristics of the 1994 cohort. After adjusting for these compositional differences, the estimated percentage of the 2005 released prisoners who were arrested within 3 years rose to 71.6%, a recidivism rate 4.7% greater than the 1994 estimate (66.9%) (table 2). However, these analyses only partially address the differences between the 1994 and 2005 studies.

## Additional Death Records on Released Prisoners Leads to Increases in Recidivism Rates

A critical difference between the 1994 and 2005 studies was the use of the Social Security Administration's public Death Master File (DMF) in the 2005 study to identify individuals who died during the follow-up period. (See *Methodology* for more information.) These individuals should be removed from the analysis because they artificially reduce the calculated recidivism rates. The 1994 study limited the identification of released prisoners who died to those who had an indication of death on their criminal history record (i.e., rap sheet).

**Table 1. Characteristics of prisoners released in 12 states in 1994 and 2005**

| Characteristic | 1994 | 2005 |
|---|---|---|
| All released prisoners | 100% | 100% |
| Sex | | |
| Male | 91.2% | 89.9% |
| Female | 8.8 | 10.1 |
| Race/Hispanic origin | | |
| White[a] | 32.2% | 35.4% |
| Black/African American[a] | 46.2 | 40.5 |
| Hispanic/Latino | 20.9 | 22.4 |
| Other[a,b] | 0.7 | 1.8 |
| Age at release | | |
| 24 or younger | 20.6% | 16.9% |
| 25–29 | 22.7 | 18.9 |
| 30–34 | 23.0 | 16.0 |
| 35–39 | 16.6 | 16.1 |
| 40 or older | 17.2 | 32.1 |
| Most serious commitment offense | | |
| Violent | 22.4% | 27.4% |
| Property | 33.2 | 29.1 |
| Drug | 33.0 | 31.4 |
| Public order[c] | 11.4 | 12.1 |
| Number of released prisoners | 249,657 | 286,829 |

Note: Estimates based on a sample of 29,387 prisoners released in 1994 and a sample of 34,649 prisoners released in 2005 in the 12 states that participated in both studies (California, Florida, Maryland, Michigan, Minnesota, New Jersey, New York, North Carolina, Ohio, Oregon, Texas, and Virginia). Data on the sex of prisoners released in 1994 were known for 100% of cases, race and Hispanic origin for 99.9%, and age at release for nearly 100%. Data on the sex of prisoners released in 2005 were known for 100% of cases, race and Hispanic origin for 99.8%, and age at release for 100%. See appendix table 1 for standard errors.

[a] Excludes persons of Hispanic or Latino origin.

[b] Includes persons identified as American Indian or Alaska Native; Asian, Native Hawaiian, or other Pacific Islander; and persons of other races. cIncludes cases in which the prisoner's most serious offense was unspecified. Source: Bureau of Justice Statistics, Recidivism of State Prisoners Released in 1994 and 2005 data collections.

The 2005 study supplemented the death information obtained from the FBI's Interstate Identification Index (III) with the DMF data. Based on both sources of information, 1,595 of the 70,878 inmates sampled for the 2005 study had died during the 5-year follow-up period. Less than 10% of those deaths were captured in the fingerprint verified death information that criminal justice agencies submitted to the FBI's III system. If the DMF data had not been used in the 2005 study and the rap sheets of these individuals had been included in the analyses, the estimated 5-year recidivism rate would have been about one-half of one percent lower.

## Effects of the Criminal History Record Improvements on Recidivism Research Are Difficult to Quantify

Direct comparisons between the published recidivism rates from the 1994 and the new 2005 study are also difficult due to the completeness of the criminal history records available to BJS at the time of the data collections. Both studies were based on fingerprint-verified automated rap sheets stored in the FBI and the state repositories. While both studies relied on records within the FBI's III system for information on the arrests and prosecutions that occurred outside of the states that released the inmates, the 2005 study used new data collection capabilities to directly access the criminal history record systems of all 50 states and obtain more comprehensive out-of-state information than what was available for the 1994 study. (See *Methodology* for more information.) In addition, BJS was unable to obtain any out-of-state criminal history information on the prisoners released in one state in the 1994 study due to a nondisclosure agreement.

**Table 2. Population-adjusted percent of prisoners arrested for a new crime within 3 years following release in 12 states in 1994 and 2005, by demographic characteristics and most serious commitment offense**

| Characteristic | 1994 | 2005[a] |
|---|---|---|
| All released prisoners | 66.9% | 71.6%** |
| Sex | | |
| Male | 67.8% | 72.5%** |
| Female | 57.2 | 62.9** |
| Race/Hispanic origin | | |
| White[b] | 61.7% | 68.8%** |
| Black/African American[b] | 71.9 | 74.0** |
| Hispanic/Latino | 64.6 | 70.7** |
| Otherb ,c | 53.6 | 72.6** |
| Age at release | | |
| 24 or younger | 74.7% | 78.2%** |
| 25–29 | 69.8 | 73.4** |

| Characteristic | 1994 | 2005[a] |
|---|---|---|
| 30–34 | 68.3 | 70.3 |
| 35–39 | 66.3 | 71.8** |
| 40 or older | 52.4 | 62.9** |
| Most serious commitment offense | | |
| Violent | 60.9% | 65.6%** |
| Property | 73.2 | 77.6** |
| Drug | 66.3 | 71.4** |
| Public order[d] | 62.2 | 66.9** |
| Number of released prisoners | 249,658 | 286,011 |

Source: Bureau of Justice Statistics, Recidivism of State Prisoners Released in 1994 and 2005 data collections.

Note: Estimates based on a sample of 29,387 prisoners released in 1994 and a sample of 34,649 prisoners released in 2005 in the 12 states that participated in both studies. See appendix table 2 for standard errors.

**Difference between the estimate on the 1994 cohort and the estimate on the standardized 2005 cohort was statistically significant at or above the 95% confidence interval.

[a] Estimates of inmates released in 2005 have been standardized to the distribution of inmates released in 1994 by sex, race, Hispanic origin, age at release, and most serious commitment offense. The unadjusted estimate for the 2005 cohort was 69.3%.

[b] Excludes persons of Hispanic or Latino origin.

[c] Includes persons identified as American Indian or Alaska Native; Asian, Native Hawaiian, or other Pacific Islander; and persons of other races. dIncludes cases in which the prisoner's most serious offense was unspecified.

The improved reporting of arrests and prosecutions maintained by the FBI and state repositories in the decade between the two studies also resulted in more complete documentation of the official criminal records of prisoners released in 2005. The quality of rap sheets has improved since the mid-1990s due to efforts funded by individual states and by BJS's National Criminal History Improvement Program (NCHIP), which awarded more than $500 million over this period to states for criminal history record improvements. As a result, many existing paper arrest records were automated and stored within a computerized criminal history system. Also, the growth in the use of automated fingerprint technology (e.g., livescan) reduced the proportion of illegible fingerprint images delivered to the repositories, resulting in more arrests and court adjudications being recorded on the rap sheets.

In addition, while local law enforcement agencies historically limited their criminal history repository submissions to arrests for felonies and serious misdemeanors, the reporting of less serious misdemeanors or minor infractions expanded during this time, although it is unknown whether this increase is due to changes in reporting practices or changes in the criminal behaviors of the released prisoners. In general, violent crimes are considered to be more serious than public order offenses. Among the prisoners who were arrested for a new crime within 3 years, public order offenses made up 36.0% of the first post-release arrests for the 2005 cohort, compared to 22.9% of the first post-release arrests for the 1994 cohort (table 3). Violent offenses accounted for 14.8% of the first post-release arrests for the 2005 cohort, compared to 18.8% of the first post-release arrests for the 1994 cohort.*

**Table 3. First arrest charge of prisoners arrested for a new crime within 3 years following release in 11 states in 1994 and 2005**

| Most serious arrest charge | 1994 | 2005 |
|---|---|---|
| All released prisoners | 100% | 100% |
| Violent | 18.8% | 14.8% |
| Property | 28.8 | 23.6 |
| Drug | 29.5 | 25.6 |
| Public order* | 22.9 | 36.0 |
| Estimated number of prisoners with a post-release arrest | 161,000 | 191,000 |

Note: Estimates based on a sample of 27,788 prisoners released in 1994 and a sample of 32,155 prisoners released in 2005 in the 11 states that participated in both studies and included charge descriptions in their arrest records. Number of arrests was rounded to the nearest 1,000. First arrest may include multiple charges; the most serious charge is reported in this table. See appendix table 3 for standard errors.

*Includes cases in which the prisoner's most serious offense was unspecified. Source: Bureau of Justice Statistics, Recidivism of State Prisoners Released in 1994 and 2005 data collections.

As a result of the improvements to the nation's criminal history records, the rap sheets of prisoners released in 2005 likely captured more complete offending histories than the rap sheets used in the 1994 study. These improvements would have resulted in higher observed recidivism rates in 2005 than in 1994, even if the two samples had the same true recidivism rates.

BJS conducted a test of this assumption by comparing the recidivism rates of the 1994 and 2005 samples using only new arrests for a violent offense. The logic behind this test was that, while the rap sheets for the 2005 cohort may contain more arrests overall and more arrests for minor offenses, arrests for violent offenses should be well represented in both sets of rap sheets. Using this more serious indictor of criminal behavior and controlling for cohort differences in offender demographics and most serious commitment offense, the percentage of released prisoners who were arrested for a violent crime within 3 years following release did not differ significantly between the 1994 (21.3%) and 2005 (21.8%) cohorts (table 4).

The stability in the 1994 and 2005 recidivism rates when recidivism is measured as a new arrest for a violent crime and the difference observed when recidivism is measured as a new offense for any offense raises questions about the overall consistency of rap sheet content between the 1994 and 2005 studies. More research is required to better understand the effects of rap sheet improvements on observed recidivism rates. However, given the limited empirical data currently available on the state-level changes in rap sheet content since the mid-1990s, the effects of rap sheet improvements on the observed recidivism rates cannot be quantified, and statistical adjustments for their effects cannot be made. Therefore, it is not advisable to compare the 2005 recidivism rates in this report with those found in earlier BJS reports until we have a deeper understanding of the changes in rap sheet content.

**Table 4. Population-adjusted percent of prisoners arrested for a violent crime within 3 years following release in 11 states in 1994 and 2005, by demographic characteristics and most serious commitment offense**

| Characteristic | 1994 | 2005[a] |
|---|---|---|
| All released prisoners | 21.3% | 21.8% |
| Sex | | |
| Male | 22.4% | 22.7% |
| Female | 10.2 | 13.1** |
| Race/Hispanic origin | | |
| White[b] | 16.4% | 19.3%** |
| Black/African American[b] | 26.2 | 25.3 |
| Hispanic/Latino | 18.7 | 18.5 |
| Other[b,c] | 19.0 | 18.5 |
| Age at release | | |
| 24 or younger | 28.9% | 28.6% |
| 25–29 | 23.9 | 24.8 |
| 30–34 | 21.2 | 20.1 |
| 35–39 | 17.3 | 19.5 |
| 40 or older | 12.7 | 14.3 |
| Most serious commitment offense | | |
| Violent | 27.0% | 24.8%** |

**Table 4. (Continued)**

| Characteristic | 1994 | 2005[a] |
|---|---|---|
| Property | 21.4 | 22.2 |
| Drug | 18.4 | 19.5 |
| Public order[d] | 17.9 | 21.4** |
| Number of released prisoners | 241,448 | 276,218 |

Note: Estimates based on a sample of 27,788 prisoners released in 1994 and a sample of 32,155 prisoners released in 2005 in the 11 states that participated in both studies and included charge descriptions in their arrest records. See appendix table 4 for standard errors.

**Difference between the estimate on the 1994 cohort and the estimate on the standardized 2005 cohort was statistically significant at or above the 95% confidence interval.

[a] Estimates of inmates released in 2005 have been standardized to the distribution of inmates released in 1994 by sex, race, Hispanic origin, age at release, and most serious commitment offense. The unadjusted estimate for the 2005 cohort was 20.1%.

[b] Excludes persons of Hispanic or Latino origin.

[c] Includes persons identified as American Indian or Alaska Native; Asian, Native Hawaiian, or other Pacific Islander; and persons of other races. dIncludes cases in which the prisoner's most serious offense was unspecified. Source: Bureau of Justice Statistics, Recidivism of State Prisoners Released in 1994 and 2005 data collections.

## Criminal History and Prison Records Were Used to Document Recidivism Patterns

This study estimates the recidivism patterns of 404,638 persons released in 2005 from state prisons in 30 states. In 2005, these states held 76% of the U.S. population and were responsible for 77% of the prisoners released from U.S. prisons (not shown). A representative sample of inmates released in 2005 was developed for each of the 30 states using data reported by state departments of corrections to BJS's National Corrections Reporting Program (NCRP), yielding a final sample of 68,597 persons. (For a complete description of the sampling and weighting procedures, see *Methodology*.) Using information contained in state and federal criminal history records (i.e., rap sheets) and the records of state departments of corrections, this report details the arrest, adjudication, conviction, and incarceration experiences of these former inmates within and outside of the state that released them for a 5-year period following their release from prison.

This research has attempted to minimize the effect on recidivism statistics posed by state variations in criminal history reporting policies, coding practices, and coverage. The analysis excluded arrest events in the rap sheets that were not commonly recorded by all states (e.g., arrests for many types of traffic offenses). The analysis also excluded sections of the rap sheets that recorded the issuance of a warrant as an arrest event when no arrest actually occurred. Some variations in the content of rap sheets remained and cannot be remediated, such as the nature of the charging decision. For example, when an inmate on parole is arrested for committing a burglary, some local law enforcement agencies coded the arrest offense as a parole violation, some coded it as a burglary, and others coded both the burglary and the parole violation. Given that this is often a local coding decision, it is difficult to discern from the contents of the rap sheets which charging approach was employed at each arrest.

Along with these coding variations, it is commonly assumed that the information derived from criminal history repositories understates the criminal histories of offenders, especially information on actions that occurred over 20 years ago. While it cannot be quantified at this time, the common perception is that, through targeted funding and the efforts of criminal justice practitioners across the country, the quality and completeness of rap sheets has improved so that they provide better assessments of recidivism patterns.

Among the 404,638 prisoners released in 30 states in 2005, 31.8% were in prison for a drug offense, 29.8% for a property offense, 25.7% for a violent offense, and 12.7% for a public order offense (table 5). Nearly 9 in 10 (89.3%) of released prisoners were male. More than a third (36.9%) of these persons were under age 30 at release, and about a third (31.5%) were age 40 or older. The proportions of non-Hispanic black (40.1%) and non-Hispanic white (39.9%) prisoners were similar. An estimated 25.7% of the released prisoners had 4 or fewer prior arrests, while 43.2% had 10 or more. Half of the released prisoners had 3 or more prior convictions.

**Table 5. Characteristics of prisoners released in 30 states in 2005**

| Characteristic | Percent |
|---|---|
| All released prisoners | 100% |
| Sex | |
| Male | 89.3% |

**Table 5. (Continued)**

| Characteristic | Percent |
|---|---|
| Female | 10.7 |
| Race/Hispanic origin | |
| White[a] | 39.9% |
| Black/African American[a] | 40.1 |
| Hispanic/Latino | 17.7 |
| Other[a,b] | 2.4 |
| Age at release | |
| 24 or younger | 17.6% |
| 25–29 | 19.3 |
| 30–34 | 15.9 |
| 35–39 | 15.7 |
| 40 or older | 31.5 |
| Most serious commitment offense | |
| Violent | 25.7% |
| Property | 29.8 |
| Drug | 31.8 |
| Public order[c] | 12.7 |
| Number of prior arrests per released prisoner[d] | |
| 2 or fewer | 11.5% |
| 3–4 | 14.2 |
| 5–9 | 31.1 |
| 10 or more | 43.2 |
| Mean number | 10.6 |
| Median number | 7.8 |
| Number of prior convictions per released prisoner[d] | |
| Mean number | 4.9 |
| Median number | 3.1 |
| Number of released prisoners | 404,638 |

Source: Bureau of Justice Statistics, Recidivism of State Prisoners Released in 2005 data collection.

Note: Data on the prisoner's sex were known for 100% of cases, race and Hispanic origin for nearly 100%, and age at release for 100%. See appendix table 5 for standard errors.

[a] Excludes persons of Hispanic or Latino origin.

[b] Includes persons identified as American Indian or Alaska Native; Asian, Native Hawaiian, or other Pacific Islander; and persons of other races.

[c] Includes 0.8% of cases in which the prisoner's most serious offense was unspecified.

[d] Includes arrest and conviction that resulted in the imprisonment.

## 1 In 10 State Prisoners Had an Out-Of-State Arrest Within 5 Years of Release

An estimated 24.7% of the released prisoners had a prior arrest in a state other than the one that released them (table 6). About 1 in 10 (10.9%) released prisoners were arrested at least once outside the state that released them during the 5-year follow-up period. These statistics show the limitations of recidivism studies that only have access to in-state criminal history information.

## 3 in 4 State Prisoners Were Arrested Within 5 Years of Release

Within 1 year after their release from state prison, 43.4% of prisoners had been arrested either in or outside of the state that released them. This percentage grew each year, increasing to 59.5% by the end of the second year, 67.8% by the end of the third year, and 76.6% by the end of the 5-year follow-up period.

Another way to view these recidivism statistics is to consider how quickly those who recidivated actually did so. More than a third (36.8%) of all released prisoners who were arrested within 5 years of release were arrested within the first 6 months, with more than half (56.7%) arrested by the end of the first year (not shown).

The longer released prisoners went without being arrested, the less likely they were to be arrested within the 5-year period. For example, compared to the arrest rate of 43.4% in the first year after release, 28.5% of persons not arrested in the first year were arrested for the first time in the second year following their release from prison (figure 2). Similarly, for those not arrested by the end of the second year, 20.5% were arrested by the end of the third year, with the arrest rate falling to 16.1% in the fourth year. Finally, 13.3% of released prisoners who went 4 years without an arrest were arrested in the fifth year.

The 404,638 persons released in 2005 were arrested an estimated 1,173,000 times in the 5 years after release (table 7). While some of them had a large number of arrests in the follow-up period (maximum of 81), most did not. Among all released prisoners, the average number of arrests in the 5-year period was 2.9, while the median number of arrests was 1.5. About 2 in 5 (42.3%) of all releasees were arrested no more than once in the 5-year period, and more than half (57.6%) had fewer than 3 arrests in the 5 years following their release.

**Table 6. Out-of-state arrests of prisoners released in 30 states in 2005**

| Out-of-state arrests | Percent |
|---|---|
| Prior to release | |
| 1 or more | 24.7% |
| 1–4 | 17.5 |
| 5–9 | 4.3 |
| 10 or more | 2.9 |
| Post-release 1 or more | 10.9% |
| 1–4 | 9.6 |
| 5–9 | 1.1 |
| 10 or more | 0.2 |

Source: Bureau of Justice Statistics, Recidivism of State Prisoners Released in 2005 data collection.

Note: Prisoners were tracked for 5 years following release. Arrested out-of-state includes arrests that occurred in states other than the one that released the prisoner in 2005. See appendix table 6 for standard errors.

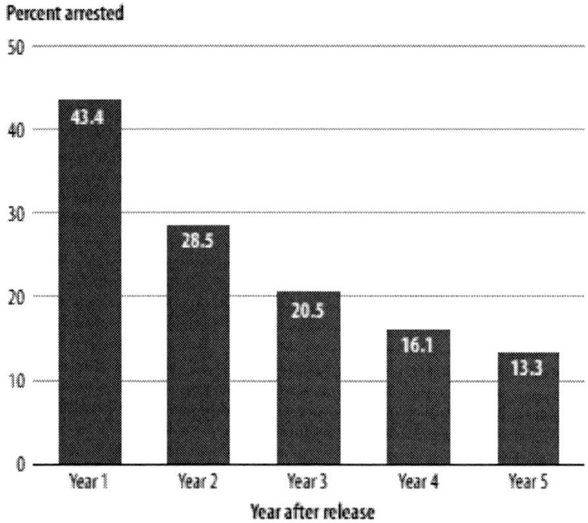


Source: Bureau of Justice Statistics, Recidivism of State Prisoners Released in 2005 data collection.

Note: The denominators for the annual rates were 404,638 for year 1; 229,035 for year 2; 163,679 for year 3; 130,128 for year 4; and 109,186 for year 5. The numerators include persons arrested in the year who had not been arrested since release. See appendix table 7 for standard errors.

Figure 2. Percent of prisoners arrested during the year who had not been arrested since release in 30 states in 2005.

Despite this, among released prisoners who were arrested at least once during the 5-year follow-up period, three-quarters (75.4%) were arrested again during the 5-year period (not shown). About a sixth (16.1%) of released prisoners were responsible for about half (48.4%) of the 1,173,000 arrests of released prisoners that occurred in the 5-year follow-up period.

**Table 7. Post-release arrests of prisoners released in 30 states in 2005**

| Post-release arrests | Percent |
|---|---|
| All released prisoners | 100% |
| None | 23.4 |
| 1 | 18.9 |
| 2 | 15.3 |
| 3 | 11.5 |
| 4 | 8.5 |
| 5 | 6.4 |
| 6 or more | 16.1 |
| Estimated number of post-release arrests | 1,173,000 |
| Mean number per released prisoner | 2.9 |
| Median number per released prisoner | 1.5 |
| Number of released prisoners | 404,638 |

Source: Bureau of Justice Statistics, Recidivism of State Prisoners Released in 2005 data collection. Source: Bureau of Justice Statistics, Recidivism of State Prisoners Released in 2005 data collection.

Note: Prisoners were tracked for 5 years following release. Number of post-release arrests was rounded to the nearest 1,000. See appendix table 8 for standard errors.

## Prisoners Released After Serving Time for a Property Offense Were the Most Likely to Be Arrested

Within 5 years of release, 82.1% of prisoners who had been committed for a property offense had been arrested for a new offense, followed by 76.9% of those committed for a drug offense (figure 3 and table 8). Offenders sentenced for a violent (71.3%) or public order offense (73.6%) were the least likely to be arrested after release.

This general pattern of recidivism was maintained across the 5-year follow-up period. A year after release from prison, the recidivism rate of prisoners sentenced for a property offense (50.3 %) was higher than the rates for drug (42.3%), public order (40.1%), and violent (38.4%) offenders. Among violent offenders, the annual recidivism rates of prisoners sentenced for homicide or sexual assault were lower than those sentenced for assault or robbery across the 5-year period. Among property offenders, inmates committed for larceny or motor vehicle theft had higher annual recidivism rates than those committed for fraud or forgery across the 5-year period.

**Table 8. Recidivism of prisoners released in 30 states in 2005, by most serious commitment offense and time from release to first arrest**

| | | *Cumulative percent of released prisoners arrested within—* | | | | |
|---|---|---|---|---|---|---|
| *Most serious commitment offense* | *6 months* | *1 year* | *2 years* | *3 years* | *4 years* | *5 years* |
| *All released prisoners* | 28.2% | 43.4% | 59.5% | 67.8% | 73.0% | 76.6% |
| *Violent* | 24.9% | 38.4% | 53.8% | 61.6% | 67.2% | 71.3% |
| Homicide[a] | 12.5 | 21.5 | 33.9 | 41.5 | 47.0 | 51.2 |
| Murder | 10.1 | 18.8 | 30.4 | 37.8 | 43.6 | 47.9 |
| Nonnegligent manslaughter | 17.3 | 27.7 | 39.4 | 46.0 | 51.5 | 55.7 |
| Negligent manslaughter | 13.2 | 21.9 | 35.5 | 43.7 | 48.8 | 53.0 |
| Rape/sexual assault | 20.8 | 30.9 | 43.7 | 50.9 | 56.0 | 60.1 |
| Robbery | 25.8 | 41.0 | 58.6 | 66.9 | 72.8 | 77.0 |
| Assault | 27.9 | 42.6 | 58.9 | 67.1 | 72.9 | 77.1 |
| Other | 28.7 | 43.4 | 56.6 | 63.0 | 66.9 | 70.4 |
| *Property* | 33.6% | 50.3% | 66.7% | 74.5% | 79.1% | 82.1% |
| Burglary | 31.0 | 48.7 | 65.8 | 73.9 | 78.9 | 81.8 |
| Larceny/motor vehicle theft | 39.3 | 56.2 | 70.8 | 77.6 | 81.6 | 84.1 |
| Fraud/forgery | 27.7 | 42.2 | 60.0 | 68.6 | 73.2 | 77.0 |
| Other | 33.2 | 49.5 | 66.6 | 75.5 | 80.9 | 83.6 |
| *Drug* | 26.9% | 42.3% | 59.1% | 67.9% | 73.3% | 76.9% |
| Possession | 28.7 | 44.5 | 60.7 | 69.6 | 75.2 | 78.3 |
| Trafficking | 26.9 | 41.5 | 58.0 | 66.6 | 71.9 | 75.4 |
| Other | 25.3 | 41.4 | 59.3 | 68.3 | 73.6 | 78.1 |
| *Public order* | 25.6% | 40.1% | 55.6% | 64.7% | 69.9% | 73.6% |
| Weapons | 35.3 | 49.1 | 65.1 | 73.1 | 76.9 | 79.5 |
| Driving under the influence | 11.9 | 22.1 | 37.2 | 48.0 | 54.9 | 59.9 |
| Other[b] | 27.8 | 44.9 | 60.4 | 69.2 | 74.1 | 77.9 |

Source: Bureau of Justice Statistics, Recidivism of State Prisoners Released in 2005 data collection.

Note: Prisoners were tracked for 5 years following release. Inmates could have been in prison for more than one offense; the most serious one is reported in this table.

See appendix table 9 for standard errors.

[a] Includes cases in which the type of homicide was unspecified, not shown separately.

[b] Includes 0.8% of cases in which the prisoner's most serious offense was unspecified.

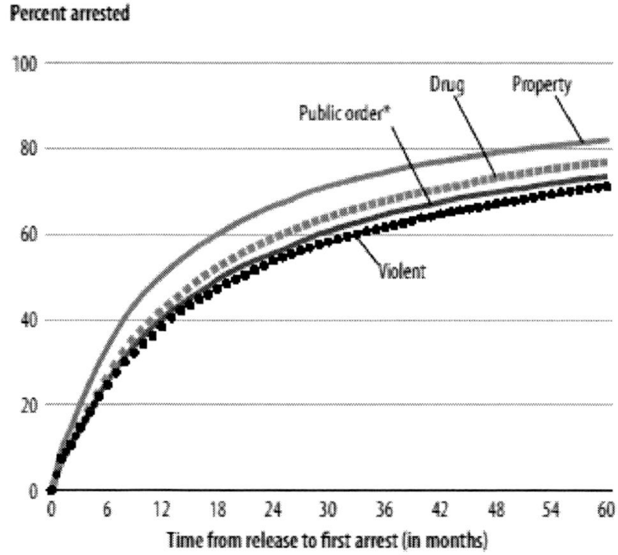


Note: Prisoners were tracked for 5 years following release.

*Includes 0.8% of cases in which the prisoner's most serious offense was unspecified.

Source: Bureau of Justice Statistics, Recidivism of State Prisoners Released in 2005 data collection.

Figure 3. Recidivism of prisoners released in 30 states in 2005, by most serious commitment offense and time from release to first arrest.

Within the first 5 years of release from state prison in 2005, an estimated 28.6% of inmates were arrested for a violent offense (table 9). Among all released inmates, an estimated 1.7% were arrested for rape or sexual assault, and 23.0% were arrested for assault. During the 5-year follow-up period, the majority (58.0%) of released prisoners were arrested for a public order offense. About 1 in 4 (25.3%) released prisoners were arrested for a probation or parole violation. An estimated 39.9% were arrested for some other public order offense, including failure to appear and obstruction of justice, which in some jurisdictions may be the legal response to probation or parole violations. Other public order offenses include drunkenness, disorderly conduct, liquor law violation, or a family-related offense.

Compared to inmates incarcerated for a property (28.5%), drug (24.8%), or public order offense (29.2%), a higher percentage of inmates incarcerated for a violent offense were arrested for another violent crime (33.1%) during the 5-year period (table 10). A higher percentage of released property offenders were arrested for a property crime (54.0%) than violent, drug, or

While recidivism rates increased through the fifth year for both released inmates with 4 or fewer prior arrests and those with 10 or more prior arrests, both groups consistently differed about 30% by the end of the first year. This general pattern remained through the next 4 years. For example, 60.8% of released inmates with 4 or fewer arrests in their prior criminal history had been arrested by the end of the fifth year, compared to 86.5% of released inmates who had 10 or more prior arrests. This finding suggests that the effect of criminal history on recidivism is observable within a year after release and continues into the future.

The negative effect of criminal history on recidivism held across the inmate's most serious incarceration offense category. Inmates incarcerated for a violent offense who had 4 or fewer arrests in their prior criminal history were less likely to be arrested within 5 years (56.3%) than those with 10 or more prior arrests (85.6%) (table 11). This disparity was also observed among violent offenders arrested within a year of release from prison, as 23.8% of inmates incarcerated for a violent offense were arrested within a year of release, compared to 55.4% of those with 10 or more prior arrests.

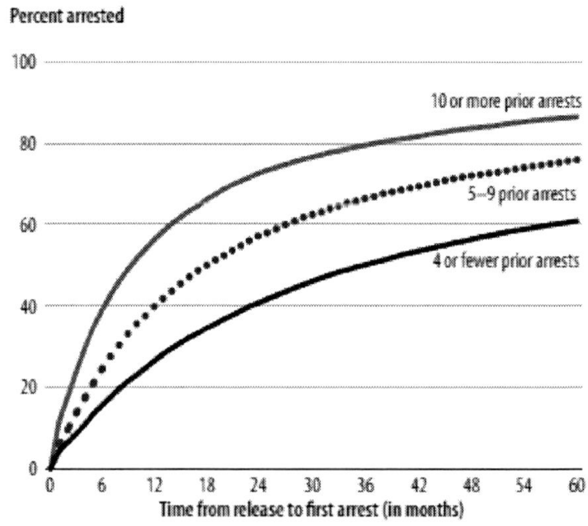


Source: Bureau of Justice Statistics, Recidivism of State Prisoners Released in 2005 data collection.

Note: Prisoners were tracked for 5 years following release. Prior arrest history includes the number of times the prisoner was arrested prior to his or her date of release.

Figure 4. Recidivism of prisoners released in 30 states in 2005, by prior arrest history and time from release to first arrest.

**Table 11. Recidivism of prisoners released in 30 states in 2005, by prior arrest history, most serious commitment offense, and time from release to first arrest**

| Prior arrest history and most serious commitment offense | | Cumulative percent of released prisoners arrested within— | | | | |
|---|---|---|---|---|---|---|
| | 6 months | 1 year | 2 years | 3 years | 4 years | 5 years |
| All released prisoners | 28.2% | 43.4% | 59.5% | 67.8% | 73.0% | 76.6% |
| 4 or fewer | 15.5% | 26.4% | 40.7% | 50.0% | 56.3% | 60.8% |
| Violent | 14.2 | 23.8 | 36.5 | 45.3 | 51.7 | 56.3 |
| Property | 18.3 | 31.4 | 47.2 | 57.4 | 63.8 | 67.9 |
| Drug | 14.8 | 25.1 | 40.8 | 50.1 | 56.4 | 61.2 |
| Public order* | 15.9 | 28.2 | 41.4 | 50.8 | 56.2 | 60.2 |
| 5–9 | 24.3% | 39.8% | 57.1% | 66.3% | 72.0% | 75.9% |
| Violent | 23.9 | 38.0 | 55.8 | 64.8 | 70.4 | 74.2 |
| Property | 28.5 | 46.2 | 63.1 | 71.8 | 76.9 | 80.5 |
| Drug | 21.6 | 37.0 | 55.7 | 65.5 | 71.6 | 75.5 |
| Public order* | 22.6 | 36.5 | 50.5 | 59.9 | 65.9 | 70.5 |
| 10 or more | 38.6% | 56.1% | 72.5% | 79.5% | 83.7% | 86.5% |
| Violent | 38.1 | 55.4 | 71.7 | 77.3 | 81.7 | 85.6 |
| Property | 42.3 | 59.9 | 76.2 | 82.5 | 86.2 | 88.3 |
| Drug | 37.0 | 55.0 | 71.1 | 78.8 | 83.3 | 86.2 |
| Public order* | 33.4 | 49.5 | 67.6 | 76.2 | 80.6 | 83.5 |

Source: Bureau of Justice Statistics, Recidivism of State Prisoners Released in 2005 data collection.

Note: Prisoners were tracked for 5 years following release. Inmates could have been in prison for more than one offense; the most serious one is reported in this table. Prior arrest history includes the number of times the prisoner was arrested prior to his or her date of release. See appendix table 12 for standard errors.

*Includes 0.8% of cases in which the prisoner's most serious offense was unspecified.

## Male Inmates Were Arrested at Higher Rates Than Female Inmates Following Release

Within 3 years of release from prison, 69.0% of male and 58.5% of female inmates had been arrested at least once (figure 5 and table 12). Five years after release from prison, more than three-quarters (77.6%) of males and two-thirds (68.1%) of females had been arrested. At the end of the first year, the male recidivism rate (44.5%) was about 10 percentage points higher than the female rate (34.4%), a difference that remained relatively stable over the following 4 years.

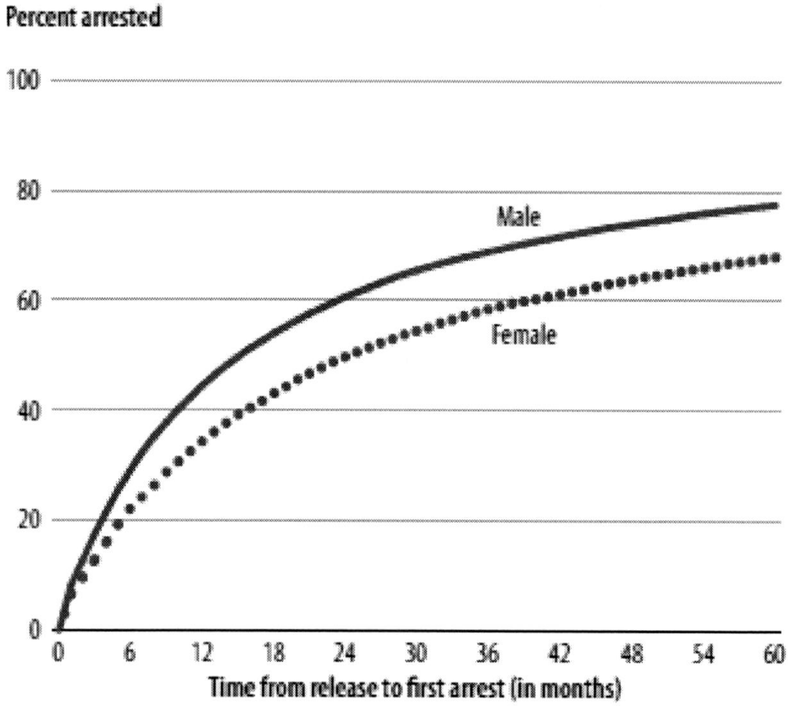


Source: Bureau of Justice Statistics, Recidivism of State Prisoners Released in 2005 data collection.

Note: Prisoners were tracked for 5 years following release. Data on prisoner's sex were known for 100% of cases.

Figure 5. Recidivism of prisoners released in 30 states in 2005, by sex of releasee and time from release to first arrest.

Among all released prisoners, the average number of arrests in the 5-year period was 2.9 for males and 2.5 for females, while the median number of arrests was 1.6 for males and 1.0 for females (table 13). Half (50.6%) of released females and about 41.3% of released males were arrested no more than once in the 5-year period, while 64.2% of females and 56.8% of males had 2 or fewer arrests over the same period.

The recidivism rates (as measured by arrests) for males were higher than those for females, regardless of the incarceration offense or the recidivism period. At the end of the 5-year follow-up period, the post-release arrest rate for both males and females was highest among those incarcerated for a property offense.

**Table 12. Recidivism of prisoners released in 30 states in 2005, by sex of releasee, most serious commitment offense, and time from release to first arrest**

| Sex of releasee and most | | | Cumulative percent of released prisoners arrested within— | | | |
|---|---|---|---|---|---|---|
| serious commitment offense | 6 months | 1 year | 2 years | 3 years | 4 years | 5 years |
| All released prisoners | 28.2% | 43.4% | 59.5% | 67.8% | 73.0% | 76.6% |
| Male | 28.9% | 44.5% | 60.7% | 69.0% | 74.1% | 77.6% |
| Violent | 25.2 | 38.9 | 54.4 | 62.3 | 67.9 | 72.0 |
| Property | 35.1 | 52.3 | 68.6 | 76.4 | 80.9 | 83.6 |
| Drug | 27.6 | 43.6 | 60.7 | 69.4 | 74.8 | 78.4 |
| Public order* | 26.1 | 40.8 | 56.3 | 65.4 | 70.5 | 74.2 |
| Female | 22.1% | 34.4% | 49.8% | 58.5% | 63.9% | 68.1% |
| Violent | 19.8 | 30.6 | 44.2 | 51.9 | 56.9 | 60.8 |
| Property | 23.8 | 37.6 | 54.3 | 62.6 | 68.0 | 72.1 |
| Drug | 21.9 | 33.3 | 48.1 | 57.6 | 62.9 | 67.3 |
| Public order* | 19.2 | 31.0 | 47.6 | 56.1 | 62.2 | 66.5 |

Source: Bureau of Justice Statistics, Recidivism of State Prisoners Released in 2005 data collection.

Note: Prisoners were tracked for 5 years following release. Inmates could have been in prison for more than one offense; the most serious one is reported in this table. Data on prisoner's sex were known for 100% of cases. See appendix table 13 for standard errors.

*Includes 0.8% of cases in which the prisoner's most serious offense was unspecified.

**Table 13. Post-release arrests of prisoners released in 30 states in 2005, by sex of releasee**

| Post-release arrests | Male | Female |
|---|---|---|
| All released prisoners | 100% | 100% |
| None | 22.4 | 31.9 |
| 1 | 18.9 | 18.7 |
| 2 | 15.5 | 13.6 |
| 3 | 11.7 | 9.5 |
| 4 | 8.7 | 6.9 |
| 5 | 6.4 | 5.8 |
| 6 or more | 16.4 | 13.5 |
| Estimated number of post-release arrests | 1,065,000 | 108,000 |
| Mean number | 2.9 | 2.5 |
| Median number | 1.6 | 1.0 |

**Table 13. (Continued)**

| Post-release arrests | Male | Female |
|---|---|---|
| Number of released prisoners | 361,469 | 43,170 |

Source: Bureau of Justice Statistics, Recidivism of State Prisoners Released in 2005 data collection.

Note: Prisoners were tracked for 5 years following release. Number of post-release arrests was rounded to the nearest 1,000. Data on prisoner's sex were known for 100% of cases. See appendix table 14 for standard errors.

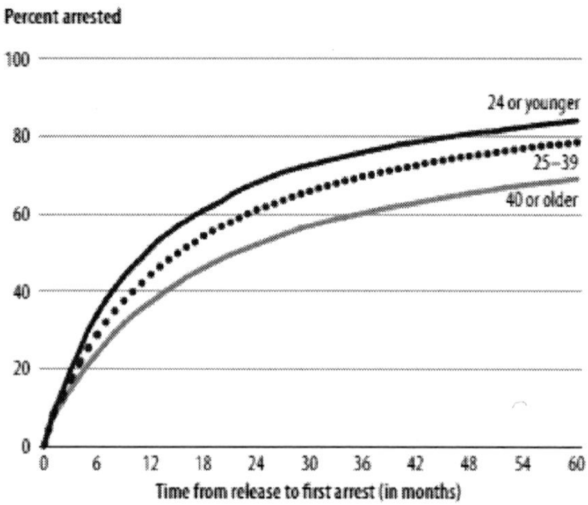


Note: Prisoners were tracked for 5 years following release. Data on prisoner's age were known for 100% of cases.

Source: Bureau of Justice Statistics, Recidivism of State Prisoners Released in 2005 data collection.

Figure 6. Recidivism of prisoners released in 30 states in 2005, by age at release and time from release to first arres.

## Younger Released Inmates Were Arrested at Higher Rates Than Older Inmates Following Release

Three years after release, 75.9% of inmates who were age 24 or younger at the time of their release had been arrested for a new offense, compared to 69.7% of those ages 25 to 39 and 60.3% of those age 40 or older (figure 6 and table 14). These patterns were still evident by the end of the fifth year. At the end of the 5-year recidivism period, 84.1% of inmates released at age 24 or younger had been arrested for a new offense, compared to 78.6% of those ages 25 to 39 and 69.2% of those age 40 or older.

**Table 14. Recidivism of prisoners released in 30 states in 2005, by age at release, most serious commitment offense, and time from release to first arrest**

| Age at release and most serious commitment offense | | Cumulative percent of released prisoners arrested within— | | | | |
|---|---|---|---|---|---|---|
| | 6 months | 1 year | 2 years | 3 years | 4 years | 5 years |
| All released prisoners | 28.2% | 43.4% | 59.5% | 67.8% | 73.0% | 76.6% |
| 24 or younger | 34.0% | 51.3% | 68.1% | 75.9% | 80.7% | 84.1% |
| Violent | 30.6 | 45.6 | 62.7 | 71.1 | 76.2 | 80.4 |
| Property | 37.3 | 55.1 | 70.9 | 78.3 | 82.9 | 85.8 |
| Drug | 31.6 | 50.0 | 69.3 | 77.4 | 82.4 | 85.4 |
| Public order* | 38.2 | 56.2 | 69.8 | 76.2 | 80.8 | 84.7 |
| 25–29 | 29.0% | 45.4% | 62.1% | 71.1% | 76.6% | 80.3% |
| Violent | 25.1 | 39.6 | 56.5 | 66.4 | 72.7 | 76.7 |
| Property | 34.2 | 51.1 | 67.3 | 75.4 | 80.0 | 83.5 |
| Drug | 27.4 | 44.3 | 61.5 | 70.8 | 76.6 | 80.4 |
| Public order* | 30.0 | 48.1 | 64.3 | 72.1 | 77.0 | 80.7 |
| 30–34 | 28.0% | 43.4% | 60.0% | 68.1% | 73.4% | 77.0% |
| Violent | 25.1 | 38.6 | 54.9 | 62.4 | 68.2 | 72.0 |
| Property | 33.8 | 50.9 | 68.3 | 76.0 | 80.7 | 83.7 |
| Drug | 25.5 | 41.2 | 58.4 | 66.8 | 72.2 | 76.1 |
| Public order* | 27.5 | 42.3 | 56.4 | 66.0 | 71.2 | 75.2 |
| 35–39 | 29.2% | 44.4% | 61.2% | 69.8% | 74.7% | 78.1% |
| Violent | 26.7 | 42.1 | 59.6 | 66.1 | 70.6 | 74.0 |
| Property | 35.0 | 52.8 | 69.3 | 77.6 | 81.9 | 83.8 |
| Drug | 27.8 | 40.7 | 56.7 | 67.0 | 72.8 | 77.0 |
| Public order* | 24.1 | 38.0 | 56.0 | 64.9 | 70.3 | 74.8 |
| 40 or older | 24.0% | 37.3% | 52.1% | 60.3% | 65.5% | 69.2% |
| Violent | 20.3 | 31.5 | 43.4 | 50.3 | 56.0 | 60.7 |
| Property | 29.8 | 44.9 | 61.2 | 69.0 | 73.8 | 76.9 |
| Drug | 24.6 | 38.7 | 54.2 | 62.5 | 67.6 | 71.2 |
| Public order* | 17.6 | 28.8 | 44.4 | 55.3 | 60.6 | 63.9 |

Source: Bureau of Justice Statistics, Recidivism of State Prisoners Released in 2005 data collection.

Note: Prisoners were tracked for 5 years following release. Inmates could have been in prison for more than one offense; the most serious one is reported in this table.

Data on prisoner's age were known for 100% of cases. See appendix table 15 for standard errors.

*Includes 0.8% of cases in which the prisoner's most serious offense was unspecified.

## By The End of the Fifth Year After Release, Black Inmates Had the Highest Recidivism Rate Among All Racial or Ethnic Groups

One year after release from prison, non-Hispanic black (45.8%) and Hispanic (46.3%) inmates had been arrested at similar rates. In comparison, non-Hispanic white inmates (39.7%) had lower recidivism rates within the first year of release than black and Hispanic inmates (figure 7 and table 15). Over the next 4 years, the recidivism rate for Hispanics did not increase as much as that for blacks. By the end of the fifth year after release from prison, white (73.1%) and Hispanic (75.3%) offenders had lower recidivism rates than black offenders (80.8%).

From at least 6 months after release from prison through the end of the 5-year follow-up period, black offenders had higher rates of recidivism than white offenders. This pattern generally held, regardless of the type of offense for which the inmate was imprisoned. Three years after release, 55.6% of white inmates who were imprisoned for a violent crime had been arrested for a new offense, compared to 66.4% of black inmates. By the end of the fifth year after release, these proportions for inmates who were imprisoned for a violent crime increased to 65.1% for white and 76.9% for black inmates.

**Table 15. Recidivism of prisoners released in 30 states in 2005, by race or Hispanic origin, most serious commitment offense, and time from release to first arrest**

| Race/Hispanic origin and most | | Cumulative percent of released prisoners arrested within— | | | | |
|---|---|---|---|---|---|---|
| serious commitment offense | 6 months | 1 year | 2 years | 3 years | 4 years | 5 years |
| All released prisoners | 28.2% | 43.4% | 59.5% | 67.8% | 73.0% | 76.6% |
| White[a] | 25.6% | 39.7% | 55.5% | 63.9% | 69.3% | 73.1% |
| Violent | 21.9 | 33.6 | 48.2 | 55.6 | 61.1 | 65.1 |
| Property | 31.2 | 47.6 | 63.9 | 71.9 | 76.9 | 80.0 |

| Race/Hispanic origin and most | | Cumulative percent of released prisoners arrested within— | | | | |
|---|---|---|---|---|---|---|
| Drug | 23.6 | 37.7 | 53.4 | 62.4 | 68.2 | 72.6 |
| Public order[b] | 21.5 | 33.9 | 50.1 | 60.2 | 65.6 | 69.5 |
| Black/African American[a] | 29.1% | 45.8% | 63.2% | 71.7% | 77.2% | 80.8% |
| Violent | 26.1 | 41.5 | 58.1 | 66.4 | 72.6 | 76.9 |
| Property | 33.9 | 51.3 | 68.5 | 76.5 | 81.8 | 84.5 |
| Drug | 28.5 | 45.5 | 63.7 | 72.6 | 77.9 | 81.5 |
| Public order[b] | 27.3 | 44.4 | 61.4 | 69.9 | 75.3 | 79.1 |
| Hispanic/Latino | 32.3% | 46.3% | 60.7% | 68.1% | 72.2% | 75.3% |
| Violent | 28.1 | 40.9 | 54.9 | 62.7 | 67.5 | 71.3 |
| Property | 39.8 | 55.7 | 71.1 | 77.6 | 80.2 | 83.0 |
| Drug | 29.0 | 42.2 | 57.0 | 65.0 | 69.8 | 72.5 |
| Public order[b] | 34.9 | 50.4 | 61.7 | 68.4 | 72.2 | 75.9 |
| Other[a,c] | 25.7% | 42.7% | 58.3% | 67.3% | 72.1% | 75.0% |
| Violent | 19.9 | 34.7 | 51.9 | 58.9 | 62.0 | 66.6 |
| Property | 36.5 | 55.4 | 69.3 | 78.3 | 81.6 | 83.7 |
| Drug | 19.4 | 39.5 | 57.0 | 67.3 | 76.5 | 78.1 |
| Public order[b] | 23.0 | 37.3 | 51.1 | 62.4 | 68.4 | 71.2 |

Source: Bureau of Justice Statistics, Recidivism of State Prisoners Released in 2005 data collection.

Note: Prisoners were tracked for 5 years following release. Inmates could have been in prison for more than one offense; the most serious one is reported in this table.

Data on the prisoner's race or Hispanic origin were known for nearly 100% of cases. See appendix table 16 for standard errors.

[a] Excludes persons of Hispanic or Latino origin.

[b] Includes 0.8% of cases in which the prisoner's most serious offense was unspecified.

[c] Includes persons identified as American Indian or Alaska Native; Asian, Native Hawaiian, or other Pacific Islander; and persons of other races.

Recidivism rates across the 5-year follow-up period for black and Hispanic inmates differed by commitment offense. For example, the recidivism rates at the end of the first year for inmates committed for a violent or drug offense were similar for both groups. By the fifth year after release, the recidivism rates for Hispanics were lower than those for blacks committed for violent or drug crimes.

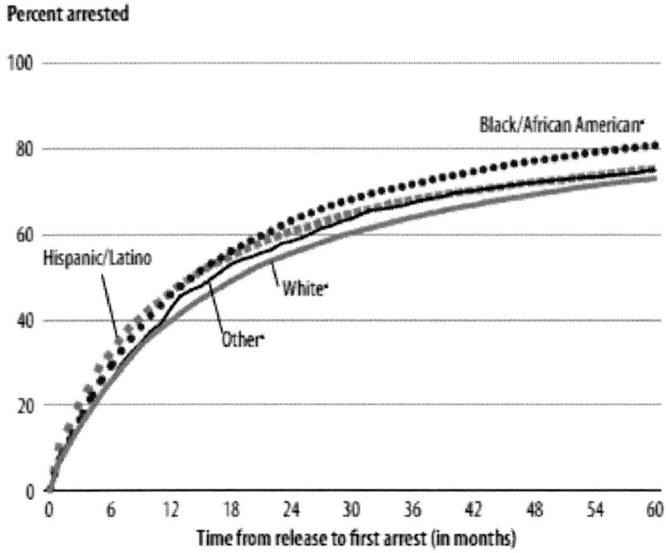


Source: Bureau of Justice Statistics, Recidivism of State Prisoners Released in 2005 data collection.

Note: Prisoners were tracked for 5 years following release. Data on prisoner's race or Hispanic origin were known for nearly 100% of cases.

[a] Excludes persons of Hispanic or Latino origin.

[b] Includes persons identified as American Indian or Alaska Native; Asian, Native Hawaiian, or other Pacific Islander; and persons of other races.

Figure 7. Recidivism of prisoners released in 30 states in 2005, by race or Hispanic origin and time from release to first arrest.

## Other Measures of Recidivism

An arrest is one of many possible measures of recidivism. In this study, four additional measures (i.e., adjudication, conviction, incarceration, and imprisonment) were prepared using criminal history records. These measures were based on prisoners released from the 29 states in the study that had the necessary data. A fifth measure —return to prison—was prepared using a combination of criminal history records and the records of state departments of corrections. This measure was based on prisoners released from 23 of the 30 states.

Because the various measures of recidivism set different criteria for labeling a person as a recidivist, the percentage of inmates classified as recidivists declined as the recidivism measurement progressed from arrest to adjudication to conviction to incarceration to imprisonment. Any use of these recidivism rates must take into account the quality and completeness of the data found in rap sheets. (See *Methodology* for more information.)

*Adjudication*—Classifies persons as a recidivist when an arrest resulted in the matter being sent deeper into the criminal justice system to be sanctioned by a court. An estimated 49.8% of inmates had an arrest within 3 years of release that resulted in the matter being referred to criminal court for adjudication, and 60.0% had an arrest within 5 years of release that resulted in an adjudication (figure 8 and table 16).

*Conviction*—Classifies persons as a recidivist if the court has determined the individual committed a new crime. An estimated 45.2% of inmates had an arrest within 3 years of release that resulted in a conviction in criminal court, and 55.4% of inmates had an arrest within 5 years that resulted in a conviction.

*Incarceration*—Classifies persons as a recidivist when an arrest resulted in a prison or jail sentence. An estimated 36.2% of inmates had an arrest within 3 years of release that resulted in a conviction with a disposition of a jail or prison sentence, compared to 44.9% within 5 years of release.

*Imprisonment*—Classifies persons as a recidivist when an arrest resulted in a prison sentence. Among inmates who had an arrest that resulted in a conviction with a disposition of a prison sentence, 22.0% were within 3 years of release, and 28.2% were within 5 years of release.

*Return to prison*—Classifies persons as a recidivist when an arrest resulted in a conviction with a disposition of a prison sentence or when the offender was returned to prison without a new conviction because of a technical violation of his or her release, such as failing a drug test or missing an appointment with a parole officer. Within 3 years of release, 49.7% of inmates either had an arrest that resulted in a conviction with a disposition of a prison sentence or were returned to prison without a new conviction because they violated a technical condition of their release, as did 55.1% of inmates within 5 years of release.

Returning to prison is probably the most common measure used in the field when studying the recidivism of released inmates. Among inmates in this study who returned to prison 1 year after release in 2005, property crime offenders (36.4%) had the highest percentage of recidivism. The 1-year returnto-prison percentages for violent (27.5%), drug (28.1%), and public order (27.7%) inmates were equal, and all were lower than that of property offenders. Five years after release from prison, the return-to-prison rate of inmates committed for a property offense (61.8%) remained higher than the return-toprison rates of inmates committed for a violent (50.6%), drug (53.3%), or public order (52.6%) offense.

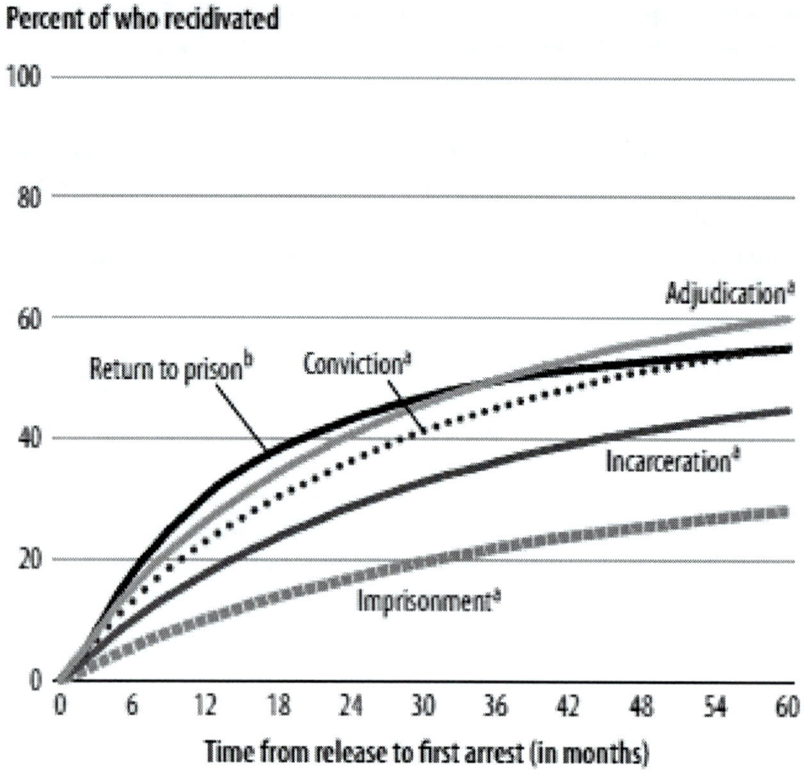


Source: Bureau of Justice Statistics, Recidivism of State Prisoners Released in 2005 data collection.

Note: Prisoners were tracked for 5 years following release in 30 states.

Some states were excluded from the specific measures of recidivism. See Methodology.

[a] Based on time from release to first arrest that led to recidivating event (i.e., adjudication, conviction, incarceration, or imprisonment) among inmates released in 29 states.

[b] Based on time from release to first arrest that led to a prison sentence or first prison admission for a technical violation without a new sentence amonginmates released in 23 states.

Figure 8. Recidivism of prisoners released in 29 states in 2005, by time from release to first arrest that led to recidivating event.

**Table 16. Recidivism of prisoners released in 29 states in 2005, by most serious commitment offense and time from release to first arrest that led to recidivating event**

| Recidivism measurement and most serious commitment offense | | Cumulative percent of released prisoners who recidivated within— | | | | |
|---|---|---|---|---|---|---|
| | 6 months | 1 year | 2 years | 3 years | 4 years | 5 years |
| Adjudication[a] | 15.2% | 26.3% | 40.7% | 49.8% | 55.9% | 60.0% |
| Violent | 11.7 | 20.6 | 33.7 | 41.7 | 48.0 | 52.6 |
| Property | 18.6 | 31.8 | 46.9 | 56.2 | 62.1 | 66.1 |
| Drug | 15.4 | 26.3 | 41.7 | 51.1 | 57.1 | 61.0 |
| Public order[b] | 14.0 | 24.7 | 38.6 | 48.4 | 54.6 | 58.5 |
| Conviction[a] | 13.0% | 23.0% | 36.3% | 45.2% | 51.3% | 55.4% |
| Violent | 9.8 | 17.6 | 29.5 | 37.2 | 43.4 | 48.0 |
| Property | 16.0 | 27.9 | 42.1 | 51.5 | 57.3 | 61.2 |
| Drug | 13.1 | 23.0 | 37.2 | 46.1 | 52.3 | 56.3 |
| Public order[b] | 12.0 | 22.2 | 34.8 | 44.7 | 50.5 | 54.2 |
| Incarceration[a] | 9.8% | 17.5% | 28.8% | 36.2% | 41.3% | 44.9% |
| Violent | 7.7 | 13.9 | 23.5 | 29.8 | 35.0 | 38.9 |
| Property | 12.1 | 21.5 | 33.5 | 41.6 | 46.9 | 50.6 |
| Drug | 9.4 | 17.0 | 29.0 | 36.1 | 41.2 | 44.6 |
| Public order[b] | 9.3 | 17.1 | 27.9 | 36.7 | 41.6 | 44.7 |
| Imprisonment[a] | 5.4% | 10.0% | 16.9% | 22.0% | 25.5% | 28.2% |
| Violent | 4.2 | 7.5 | 13.2 | 17.3 | 20.3 | 22.9 |
| Property | 7.2 | 13.0 | 20.7 | 26.5 | 30.3 | 33.4 |
| Drug | 4.8 | 9.4 | 16.4 | 21.5 | 25.1 | 27.6 |
| Public order[b] | 4.9 | 9.6 | 16.6 | 22.2 | 25.8 | 28.2 |
| Return to prison[c] | 17.6% | 30.4% | 43.3% | 49.7% | 52.9% | 55.1% |
| Violent | 16.2 | 27.5 | 39.5 | 45.4 | 48.4 | 50.6 |
| Property | 21.8 | 36.4 | 49.6 | 56.2 | 59.5 | 61.8 |
| Drug | 15.4 | 28.1 | 41.8 | 48.0 | 51.2 | 53.3 |
| Public order[b] | 16.1 | 27.7 | 39.4 | 46.7 | 50.1 | 52.6 |

Source: Bureau of Justice Statistics, Recidivism of State Prisoners Released in 2005 data collection.

Note: Prisoners were tracked for 5 years following release in 30 states. Some states were excluded from the specific measures of recidivism. See Methodology. Inmates could have been in prison for more than one offense; the most serious one is reported in this table. See appendix table 17 for standard errors.

[a] Based on time from release to first arrest that led to recidivating event (i.e., adjudication, conviction, incarceration, or imprisonment) among inmates released in 29 states.

[b] Includes 0.8% of cases in which the prisoner's most serious offense was unspecified.

[c] Based on time from release to first arrest that led to a prison sentence or first prison admission for a technical violation without a new sentence among inmates released in 23 states.

# METHODOLOGY

## Background

In 2008, the Bureau of Justice Statistics (BJS) entered into a data sharing agreement with the FBI's Criminal Justice Information Services (CJIS) Division and the International Justice and Public Safety Network (Nlets) to provide BJS access to criminal history records (i.e., rap sheets) through the FBI's Interstate Identification Index (III). A data security agreement was executed between BJS, the FBI, and Nlets to define the operational and technical practices used to protect the confidentiality and integrity of the criminal history data during exchange, processing, and storage.

The FBI's III is an automated pointer system that allows authorized agencies to determine whether any state repository has criminal history records on an individual. Nlets is a computer-based network that is responsible for the interstate transmissions of federal and state criminal history records. It allows users to query III and send requests to states holding criminal history records on an individual. The FBI also maintains criminal history records that they are solely responsible for disseminating. The identification bureaus that operate the central repositories in each state respond automatically to requests over the Nlets network. Responses received via Nlets represent an individual's national criminal history record.

Under the Criminal History Records Information Sharing (CHRIS) Project (award 2008-BJ-CX-K040), Nlets developed an automated collection system for BJS to retrieve national criminal history records from the FBI and state repositories on large samples of study subjects. Nlets produced software to parse the fields from individual criminal history records into a relational database. The database consists of state- and federal-specific numeric codes and text descriptions (e.g., criminal statutes and case outcome information) in a uniform record layout. In September 2010, BJS and Nlets conducted a pilot test of the data collection system and rap sheet parsing programs to ensure the software could handle the wide variations in the nation's criminal history records.

The Conversion of Criminal History Records into Research Databases (CCHRRD) Project (grant 2009-BJ-CX-K058) funded NORC at the University of Chicago to develop software that standardizes the content of the relational database produced by Nlets into a uniform coding structure that supports national-level recidivism research. The 2005 prisoner recidivism study was the first project to use the systems developed under the CHRIS and CCHRRD projects. The electronic records accessed by BJS through III for this study are the same records used by police officers to determine the current criminal justice status (e.g., on probation, parole, or bail) of a suspect; by judges to make pretrial and sentencing decisions; and by corrections officials to determine inmate classifications, parole releases, and work furloughs.

## Sampling

States were selected for the study based on their ability to provide prisoner records and the FBI or state identification numbers on persons released from correctional facilities in 2005. The fingerprint-based identification numbers were needed to obtain criminal history records on the released prisoners. The prisoner records—obtained from the state departments of corrections through BJS's National Corrections Reporting Program (NCRP)—also included each inmate's date of birth, sex, race, Hispanic origin, confinement offenses, sentence length, type of prison admission and release, and date of release. The 30 states that supplied BJS with the required data included Alaska, Arkansas, California, Colorado, Florida, Georgia, Hawaii, Iowa, Louisiana, Maryland, Michigan, Minnesota, Missouri, Nebraska, Nevada, New Jersey, New York, North Carolina, North Dakota, Ohio, Oklahoma, Oregon, Pennsylvania, South Carolina, South Dakota, Texas, Utah, Virginia, Washington, and West Virginia. Among each of these states, the percentage of prisoner records with a state or FBI identification number ranged from 93% to 100%, and averaged 99% (not shown).

Of the 544,728 inmates released in the study's 30 states in 2005, 412,731 met BJS's selection criteria for this study (table 17). The study excluded releases that were transfers to the custody of another authority, releases due to death, releases on bond, releases to seek or participate in an appeal of a case, and escapes from prison or absent without official leave (AWOL). Inmates whose sentence was less than 1 year were also excluded. The first release during 2005 was selected for persons released multiple times during the year.

BJS drew a systematic random sample of eligible cases from each of the 30 states. Sex was used to stratify the sampling frame within each state. The eligible cases were then separated into 16 categories based on the most serious prison commitment offense. The sampling design included all individuals who were in prison for homicide. Before selecting the sample, prison records of persons committed for a nonhomicide offense were grouped by sex, and then sorted by the county in which the sentence was imposed, race, Hispanic origin, age, and commitment offense. The sampling rate for female prisoners was doubled to improve the precision of their recidivism estimates. A total of 70,878 released prisoners were randomly selected to represent the 412,731 released in 2005 in the 30 states. Each prisoner in the sample was assigned a weight based on the probability of selection within the state.

## Collecting and processing criminal records for recidivism research

BJS received approval from the FBI's Institutional Review Board to access criminal history records through III for this study. This study employed a 5-year follow-up period, two years longer than found in previous BJS recidivism studies. In June 2011, BJS sent the state and FBI identification numbers supplied by the departments of corrections to III via Nlets to collect the criminal history records on the 70,878 former prisoners. These criminal history records contain information from the state that released them, as well as all other states in the U.S., and records covering events prior to and following their release in 2005. Over a 73-week period, Nlets electronically collated the responses received from the FBI and state criminal history repositories into a relational database.

The criminal history information on the sampled prisoners from 30 states included over 800,000 pre- and post-release arrests and dispositions from more than 25,000 criminal justice agencies in all 50 states and the District of Columbia. BJS conducted a series of data quality checks on the criminal history records to assess the accuracy and completeness of the information, beginning with an examination of the response messages and the identification numbers that failed to match a record in III. In August 2011, BJS had Nlets submit a separate set of record requests directly to the state repositories for cases in which the original request in June did not produce criminal history information. These secondary requests provided additional criminal history records that were not available through III.

To ensure that the correct records were received on the released prisoners using their fingerprint-based identification numbers, BJS compared other individual identifiers in the NCRP data to those reported in the criminal history records. A released prisoner's date of birth in the NCRP data exactly matched his or her birthdate in the criminal history records 98% of the time. Nearly 100% of the NCRP and criminal history records matched on sex and race at the person level.

This report relied on a combination of arrest charge, court disposition, incarceration sentence, and custody information to measure recidivism. Juvenile offenses were rarely included in the criminal history records unless the offender was charged or tried in court as an adult. BJS reviewed the composition of information reported in the criminal history records for distributional differences and inconsistencies in reporting practices and observed some variations across states. During the data processing and analysis phases, steps were taken to standardize the information used to measure recidivism and to minimize the impact these variations had on the overall recidivism estimates.

For example, administrative (e.g., a criminal registration or the issuance of a warrant) and procedural (e.g., transferring a suspect to another jurisdiction) records embedded in the arrest data that did not refer to an actual arrest were identified and removed from the study. Traffic violations (with the exception of vehicular manslaughter, driving while intoxicated, and hit-and-run) were also excluded from the study because the coverage of these events in the criminal history records varied widely by state.

The criminal history records from some states recorded sentence modifications that occurred after the original court disposition and sentence while records from other states did not. To ensure consistent counting rules were employed when measuring recidivism across states, the initial court disposition was captured for an arrest charge when subsequent sentence modifications were also reported within the same arrest cycle. For instance, if a court adjudication was originally deferred and then later modified to a conviction, the deferred adjudication was coded as the disposition for that arrest charge.

To assess the completeness of the adjudication and incarceration information reported in the criminal history records, BJS attempted to identify an incarceration sentence (within the state where the release occurred) in each prisoner's criminal history prior to the date of his or her most recent prison admission before being released in 2005 according to the NCRP. Overall, 93% of the cases had a criminal history record that met these criteria.

**Table 17. Number of prisoners released in 30 states in 2005**

| State | Number of released prisoners[a] | Number of sample cases | Released prisoners included in the study[b] | | Criminal history record collected | |
|---|---|---|---|---|---|---|
| | | | Weighted total | Sample size | Number | Percent |
| All released prisoners | 412,731 | 70,878 | 404,638 | 69,279 | 68,597 | 99.0% |
| Alaska | 1,827 | 1,158 | 1,764 | 1,118 | 1,099 | 98.3 |
| Arkansas | 10,844 | 2,785 | 10,513 | 2,697 | 2,640 | 97.9 |
| California | 107,633 | 4,604 | 106,116 | 4,542 | 4,541 | 100 |
| Colorado | 8,277 | 2,351 | 8,042 | 2,281 | 2,275 | 99.7 |
| Florida | 31,537 | 3,350 | 30,975 | 3,285 | 3,272 | 99.6 |
| Georgia | 12,321 | 2,763 | 12,054 | 2,697 | 2,602 | 96.5 |
| Hawaii | 1,041 | 793 | 1,022 | 779 | 772 | 99.1 |
| Iowa | 4,607 | 1,897 | 4,465 | 1,839 | 1,836 | 99.8 |
| Louisiana | 12,876 | 2,806 | 12,552 | 2,737 | 2,723 | 99.5 |
| Maryland | 10,200 | 2,597 | 9,859 | 2,513 | 2,494 | 99.2 |
| Michigan | 12,177 | 2,603 | 11,775 | 2,519 | 2,504 | 99.4 |
| Minnesota | 4,619 | 1,897 | 4,581 | 1,882 | 1,879 | 99.8 |
| Missouri | 15,997 | 2,919 | 15,513 | 2,828 | 2,823 | 99.8 |
| Nebraska | 1,386 | 966 | 1,366 | 952 | 952 | 100 |
| Nevada | 5,022 | 1,973 | 4,965 | 1,949 | 1,808 | 92.8 |
| New Jersey | 13,097 | 2,697 | 12,992 | 2,674 | 2,630 | 98.4 |
| New York | 23,963 | 3,532 | 23,448 | 3,459 | 3,459 | 100 |
| North Carolina | 11,743 | 2,748 | 11,335 | 2,653 | 2,643 | 99.6 |
| North Dakota | 884 | 686 | 868 | 674 | 666 | 98.8 |
| Ohio | 15,832 | 3,070 | 15,688 | 3,038 | 2,966 | 97.6 |
| Oklahoma | 7,768 | 2,345 | 7,459 | 2,250 | 2,184 | 97.1 |
| Oregon | 4,731 | 1,955 | 4,625 | 1,912 | 1,910 | 99.9 |
| Pennsylvania | 12,452 | 2,840 | 12,020 | 2,741 | 2,714 | 99.0 |
| South Carolina | 10,046 | 2,537 | 9,982 | 2,519 | 2,512 | 99.7 |
| South Dakota | 2,159 | 1,285 | 2,151 | 1,280 | 1,275 | 99.6 |
| Texas | 43,532 | 3,779 | 43,118 | 3,742 | 3,742 | 100 |
| Utah | 3,000 | 1,569 | 2,974 | 1,556 | 1,548 | 99.5 |
| Virginia | 12,776 | 2,719 | 12,319 | 2,619 | 2,609 | 99.6 |
| Washington | 8,439 | 2,443 | 8,234 | 2,382 | 2,380 | 99.9 |
| West Virginia | 1,945 | 1,211 | 1,864 | 1,162 | 1,139 | 98.0 |

[a] Excludes releases of prisoners whose sentence was less than 1 year, releases to custody/detainer/warrant, releases due to death, escapes or being absent without leave, transfers, administrative releases, and releases on appeal. The first release was selected for persons released multiple times during 2005.

Most criminal history records reported detailed information on the offender's adjudicated guilt or innocence and, if convicted, on the sentence imposed (e.g., prison, jail, or probation). BJS examined the disposition rates and found the proportion of arrests with a court disposition varied across states. This could be due to natural variations in state practices. However, the variations may be caused by either a lack of reporting court dispositions to the state repository or the inability of the repository to connect a reported court disposition to a specific arrest. BJS also found in some states that disposition information for certain arrests, such as arrests for failure to appear or contempt of court, was sometimes reported back on the earlier arrest for the underlying crime.

One aspect of recidivism measured in this study was a return to prison for a technical parole or other community supervision violation (e.g., failing a drug test or missing an appointment with a probation officer) or a sentence for a new crime. BJS found that the availability of the information on technical violations varied in the criminal history records by state likely because those types of returns to prison may not involve a new court sentence. Given the inconsistent reporting of such custody information in the criminal history records, the annual prison admission records from the NCRP were used to supplement the criminal history data to capture returns to prison with or without a sentence for a new crime. Analyzing the NCRP data, BJS used a set of individual identifiers (e.g., state identification number, inmate identification number, date of birth, sex, and race) to locate information on new prison admissions for a study subject during the 5 years following release in 2005. Using this information in combination with incarcerations recorded on the rap sheets, BJS identified released prisoners who returned to prison within the 5-year recidivism window.

## Adjustment of Sample Weights

### *Deaths*

BJS determined that 1,595 of the 70,878 sampled prisoners died during the 5-year follow-up period. Initial identification of sampled prisoners who died within the 5-year follow-up period was done using death information contained on the rap sheets. Additional deaths were identified by probabilistically linking sampled prisoners to individuals identified as dead in the Social Security Administration's (SSA) public Death Master File (DMF).

Specifically, linkplus, a probabilistic record linkage program developed by CDC, was used to create and score potential matches between the released prisoners' records and the public DMF, using common information found on each file (i.e., social security number (SSN), first name, last name, and date of birth (DOB))[1]. For persons with multiple SSNs, names and DOBs, all possible combinations (over 3.5 million unique permutations) were tested for matches. Based on the framework and decision rules as proposed by Fellegi and Sunter (1969), the software computed a probabilistic record linkage score for each matched record, with the score representing the sum of the agreement and disagreement weights for each matching variable; the higher the score, the greater the likelihood that the match made is a true match.[2] In order to differentiate true matches from false matches, the scores of the linked records were manually evaluated to ascertain the appropriate upper and lower bound cutoff scores. During this review, it was determined that records with a score of 20.0 or higher were exact matches of name, SSN, and DOB, and scores of less than 10.9 indicated none of the personally identifiable information matched. Accordingly, these cutoffs were used as the upper and lower cutoff scores to automatically designate true matches and nonmatches. All remaining pairs that fell between the upper and lower cutoff scores were manually reviewed by two independent reviewers and independently categorized and all discrepancies where the reviewers did not agree (less than 1%) were jointly classified.

Of importance, the number of released prisoners who were identified as dead in the DMF likely represents an undercount of the actual number of deaths within the sample. This is due, in part, to the limitations of the public DMF. Specifically, due to state disclosure laws, the public DMF does not include information on certain protected state death records (defined as records received via SSA's contracts with the states). This change, which occurred in November 2011, resulted in SSA removing over 4.2 million state-reported death records from the public DMF and adding over 1 million fewer records annually to the current public DMF thereafter. As a result, the public DMF contains an undercount of annual deaths.

It is unknown precisely how extensively the public DMF undercounts the annual number of deaths. Preliminary analyses comparing the number of deaths in the public DMF to those reported via the Centers for Disease Control and Prevention's (CDC) mortality counts suggest that in 2005 the public DMF undercounted the overall number of deaths in the United States by around 10%. The undercount has increased each year since 2005. As of 2010 the public DMF contained around half (45%) of the deaths reported by the CDC (not shown). Furthermore, the coverage of the public DMF differs by decedent age, with younger decedents being less likely to appear in the public file. Because of this, it is likely that the death count of prisoners released in 2005 is an undercount of the actual number of deaths within the sample.

The 1,595 prisoners who died during the follow-up period were excluded from the study, along with four additional cases that were later determined to be invalid release records. When weighted, these 1,599 cases represented 8,092 prison releases. Therefore, the study's sample of 69,279 eligible prisoners is statistically representative of the 404,638 prisoners released in 2005 who were identified as living for at least 5 years after their dates of release.

### *Missing Criminal History Records*

Among the 69,279 eligible prisoners sampled from 30 states, BJS did not obtain criminal history records on 406 subjects because the departments of corrections were unable to provide their FBI or state identification number. An additional 276 prisoners had an identification number, but no criminal history record linked to this number was found in the FBI or state record repositories. To account for the missing data, the original sample weights for the cases with complete criminal history information required adjustment. The sample weights for the 682 cases without a criminal history record were equally distributed among the weights of the 68,597 cases with the same commitment offense, demographic characteristics (i.e., sex, race, Hispanic origin, and age category), and state where released. The adjusted weights for the final sample of 68,597 persons were used to produce recidivism estimates on the 404,638 persons released from prison in the 30 states in 2005.

## Conducting Tests of Statistical Significance

Because this study was based on a sample and not a complete enumeration, the estimates in this report are subject to sampling error (i.e., a discrepancy between an estimate and a population parameter based on chance). One measure of the sampling error associated with an estimate is the standard error. The standard error can vary from one estimate to the next. In general, for a given metric, an estimate with a smaller standard error provides a more reliable approximation of the true value than an estimate with a larger standard error. Estimates with relatively large standard errors are associated with less precision and reliability and should be interpreted with caution. BJS conducted tests to determine whether differences in estimated numbers and percentages were statistically significant once sampling error was taken into account.

All differences discussed in this report are statistically significant at or above the 95% confidence interval. Standard errors were generated using SUDAAN, a statistical software package that estimates sampling error from complex sample surveys. Standard errors for each table are available at the end of the report.

## Computing Population-Adjusted Estimates of Recidivism for the 1994 and 2005 Studies

To examine how the recidivism rates from this study compared with those found in the previous one that measured the recidivism of prisoners released in 1994, BJS limited the comparison to the post-release arrest rates among inmates released from state prisons in the 12 states that were in both studies (California, Florida, Maryland, Michigan, Minnesota, New Jersey, New York, North Carolina, Ohio, Oregon, Texas, and Virginia). To control for the compositional differences in the types of prisoners released in these states during 1994 and 2005, RTI International (RTI) assisted BJS with standardizing the distribution of the 2005 prison release cohort to the distribution of the 1994 prison release cohort based on the following categorical variables.

- Sex (male or female)
- Age at release (24 or younger, 25 to 29, 30 to 34, 35 to 39, or 40 or older)
- Race/Hispanic origin (non-Hispanic white, non-Hispanic black, Hispanic, or other race)
- Most serious prison commitment offense (violent, property, drug, or public order).

RTI used SUDAAN software to generate the standardized estimates and determine whether any differences between the estimates for 1994 and 2005 cohorts were statistically significant. The following procedures were used to complete the analysis.

1. Missing data on the demographic characteristics and commitment offenses of the inmates were imputed using a stochastic imputation approach, which determined the cumulative distribution function (CDF) for the characteristic being imputed based on inmates with a known value for the characteristic. Inmates with a missing value were randomly assigned a value based on the CDF. For age at release, the CDF was conditioned on the sex of the inmate. For all other characteristics, the CDF was conditioned on the sex and age at release of the inmate. Data on the sex of inmates released in 1994 were known for 100% of cases, race and Hispanic origin for 99.9%, age at release for nearly 100%, and commitment offense for 99.9%. Data on sex of inmates released in 2005 were known for 100% of cases, race and Hispanic origin for 99.8%, age at release for 100%, and commitment offense for 99.8%.
2. A joint probability distribution was produced of inmates in the 1994 cohort based on sex, age at release, race/Hispanic origin, and most serious commitment offense. This distribution documented the proportion of the 1994 cohort that fell into each of 160 specific inmate subpopulations defined by crossing five categories of age, two categories of sex, four categories of race/Hispanic origin, and four categories of commitment offenses.
3. In order to allow for simultaneous estimation and comparisons, a stacked file was created containing the records on both the 1994 cohort and the 2005 cohort. A new variable (called GROUP) was created to distinguish in which cohort the inmate resided (1=1994 and 2=2005).
4. The PROC DESCRIPT procedure in SUDAAN was used to generate the standardized point estimates. This approach standardized the estimates for the 2005 cohort to the probability distribution of the 1994 cohort obtained in step 2.
   a) The standard errors for the standardized estimates were calculated in SUDAAN with a "without replacement" sample design (DESIGN = WOR).
   b) The sampling weights for the 1994 and 2005 studies were assigned in the WEIGHT statement.
   c) A single variable that accounted for the unique sample designs of the 1994 and 2005 studies was specified in the NEST statement.
   d) In the STDVAR statement, the four imputed inmate characteristic variables were listed in the order the probability distribution was

created — sex, age, race/Hispanic origin, and commitment offense. These variables were also listed in the CLASS statement.

e) The joint probability distribution of the 1994 cohort was listed in the STDWGT statement.
f) In the TABLE statement, the GROUP variable was crossed with each of the nonimputed inmate characteristics. In other words, an index combining the cohort identifier and each of the inmate characteristics was specified. This generated a separate marginal recidivism estimate for each set of inmate characteristics by cohort year.
g) The recidivism outcome variables of interest (i.e., arrested for any type of crime and arrested for a violent crime) were listed in the VAR statement.
h) The mean (MEAN) and standard error of the mean (SEMEAN) were calculated, imported into a table, and then converted into percentages by multiplying the proportions by 100.

5. The PROC DESCRIPT procedure was used to test the statistical differences for each inmate characteristic between the 1994 cohort and the standardized 2005 cohort. Using the PROC DESCRIPT procedure to conduct the test of differences allowed any correlation between the two cohort groups to be accounted for in the standard error of the test statistic.
   a) The same DESIGN, WEIGHT, NEST, STDVAR, and STDWGT statements specified in step 4 were used to conduct the statistical significance tests.
   b) The inmate characteristics were listed in the TABLE statement.
   c) The same VAR statement was used from step 4.
   d) The two levels in the GROUP variable were compared using the DIFFVAR statement.
   e) In the CATLEVEL statement, the numeric code "1" was indicated to get the percentages of inmates who had a post-release arrest within 3 years.
   f) The difference in the percentages (PERCENT), the standard error of the percentages (SEPERCENT), the test for the statistical difference (T_PCT), and the p-value for the test statistic (P_PCT) were imported into a table.
6. The p-value was used to determine which comparisons were significant at the 95% confidence interval, and those comparisons were assigned a symbol of "**."

## Recidivism Measures

This study measured six types of events to describe the recidivism of persons released from prison in 2005:

- *Arrest:* An arrest within 5 years of exiting prison in 2005. Information presented on the number of arrests is based on unique arrest dates, not individual charges.
- *Adjudication:* An arrest within 5 years of exiting prison in 2005 that resulted in a subsequent court adjudication or disposition (e.g., convictions, dismissals, acquittals, or deferred adjudications). Information on the number of adjudications is based on each unique arrest date that led to an adjudication, not the date of adjudication.
- *Conviction:* An arrest within 5 years of exiting prison in 2005 that resulted in a subsequent court conviction. Information on the number of convictions is based on each unique arrest date that led to a conviction, not the date of conviction.
- *Incarceration:* An arrest within 5 years of exiting prison in 2005 that resulted in a prison or jail sentence. Information on the number of incarcerations is based on each unique arrest date that led to a prison or jail sentence, not the date that the sentence was imposed.
- *Imprisonment:* An arrest within 5 years of exiting prison in 2005 that resulted in a prison sentence. When the type of facility (e.g., prison or jail) where an incarceration sentence was to be served was not reported in the criminal history records, a sentence of a year or more was defined as imprisonment. Information on the number of prison sentences is based on each unique arrest date that led to a prison sentence, not the date that the sentence was imposed.

The arrests that occurred within the 5-year follow-up period were tracked for an additional 6 months to determine whether the case outcomes led to an adjudication, conviction, incarceration, or imprisonment. These four measures were based on prisoners released in 29 of the study's 30 states. Louisiana prisoners were excluded because the disposition and sentencing information from that state was generally not linked to the associated arrest.

- *Return to prison:* An arrest or a technical violation of a condition of release within 5 years of exiting prison in 2005 that resulted in a return to prison. This recidivism measure incorporates the criminal history records from the FBI and state repositories and the prisoner records obtained from the state departments of corrections through the NCRP. The criminal history records provided information on arrests that resulted in incarceration during the 5-year follow-up period. BJS used the NCRP files from 2005 through 2010 to supplement the criminal history records with information on the released prisoners who returned to prison for a technical violation that did not involve a sentence for a new crime.

Prisoners released from Maryland, Nebraska, Nevada, Ohio, Pennsylvania, and Virginia were excluded from the return-to-prison analysis because the individual identifiers or complete prison admission data needed to locate returns to prison during the entire 2005 through 2010 observation window were not available. Louisiana prisoners were also excluded from the return-to-prison analysis because the sentencing information in the criminal history records from this state was generally not linked to the associated arrest.

## Offense Definitions

*Violent offenses* include homicide, rape or sexual assault, robbery, assault, and other miscellaneous or unspecified violent offenses.

*Homicide* includes murder, nonnegligent manslaughter, negligent manslaughter, and unspecified homicide offenses.

*Murder* is (1) intentionally causing the death of another person without extreme provocation or legal justification, or (2) causing the death of another while committing or attempting to commit another crime.

*Nonnegligent (or voluntary) manslaughter* is intentionally and without legal justification causing the death of another when acting under extreme provocation.

*Negligent (or involuntary) manslaughter* is causing the death of another person through recklessness or gross negligence, without intending to cause death. Negligent manslaughter also includes vehicular manslaughter, but excludes vehicular murder (intentionally killing someone with a motor vehicle), which is classified as murder.

*Rape or sexual assault* includes (1) forcible intercourse (vaginal, anal, or oral) with a female or male, (2) forcible sodomy or penetration with a foreign object (sometimes called "deviate sexual assault"), (3) forcible or violent sexual acts not involving intercourse with an adult or minor, (4) nonforcible sexual acts with a minor (such as statutory rape or incest with a minor), and (5) nonforcible sexual acts with someone unable to give legal or factual consent because of mental or physical defect or intoxication.

*Robbery* is the unlawful taking of property that is in the immediate possession of another, by force or the threat of force. Includes forcible purse snatching, but excludes nonforcible purse snatching.

*Assault* includes aggravated, simple and unspecified assault. Aggravated assault includes (1) intentionally and without legal justification causing serious bodily injury, with or without a deadly weapon, or (2) using a deadly or dangerous weapon to threaten, attempt, or cause bodily injury, regardless of the degree of injury, if any. The category also includes attempted murder, aggravated battery, felonious assault, and assault with a deadly weapon. Simple assault includes intentionally and without legal justification causing less than serious bodily injury without a deadly or dangerous weapon, or attempting or threatening bodily injury without a dangerous or deadly weapon.

*Other violent offenses* contain a range of crimes, including intimidation, illegal abortion, extortion, cruelty towards a child or wife, kidnapping, hit-and-run with bodily injury, and miscellaneous or unspecified crimes against the person.

*Property offenses* include burglary, fraud/forgery, larceny, motor vehicle theft, and other miscellaneous or unspecified property offenses.

*Burglary* is the unlawful entry of a fixed structure used for regular residence, industry, or business, with or without the use of force, to commit a felony or theft.

*Larceny* is the unlawful taking of property other than a motor vehicle from the possession of another, by stealth, without force or deceit. Includes pocket picking, nonforcible purse snatching, shoplifting, and thefts from motor vehicles. Excludes receiving or reselling stolen property or both, and thefts through fraud or deceit.

*Motor vehicle theft* is the unlawful taking of a self-propelled road vehicle owned by another. Includes the theft of automobiles, trucks, and motorcycles, but not the theft of boats, aircraft, or farm equipment (classified as larceny). Also includes receiving, possessing, stripping, transporting, and reselling stolen vehicles, and unauthorized use of a vehicle (joyriding).

*Fraud/forgery* includes using deceit or intentional misrepresentation to unlawfully deprive persons of his or her property or legal rights. It also includes offenses such as embezzlement, check fraud, confidence game, counterfeiting, and credit card fraud.

*Other property offenses* include arson, stolen property offenses, possession of burglary tools, damage to property, trespassing, and miscellaneous or unspecified property crimes.

*Drug offenses* include possession, trafficking, and other miscellaneous or unspecified drug offenses.

*Drug possession* includes possession of an illegal drug, but excludes possession with intent to sell. It also includes offenses involving drug paraphernalia and forged or unauthorized prescriptions.

*Drug trafficking* includes manufacturing, distributing, selling, smuggling, and possession with intent to sell.

*Other drug offenses* include offenses involving drug paraphernalia, forged or unauthorized prescriptions, and other miscellaneous or unspecified drug offenses.

*Public order offenses* include weapons offenses, driving under the influence, and other miscellaneous or unspecified offenses.

*Weapons offenses* include the unlawful sale, distribution, manufacture, alteration, transportation, possession, or use of a deadly or dangerous weapon or accessory.

*Driving under the influence (DIM)* is driving under the influence of drugs or alcohol and driving while intoxicated.

*Other public order offenses* are those that violate the peace or order of the community or threaten the public health or safety through unacceptable conduct, interference with governmental authority, or the violation of civil rights or liberties. The category also includes probation or parole violation, escape, obstruction of justice, court offenses, nonviolent sex offenses, commercialized vice, family offenses, liquor law violations, bribery, invasion of privacy, disorderly conduct, contributing to the delinquency of a minor, and other miscellaneous or unspecified offenses.

**Appendix Table 1. Standard errors for table 1: Characteristics of prisoners released in 12 states in 1994 and 2005**

| Characteristic | 1994 | 2005 |
|---|---|---|
| Sex | | |
| Male | 0.28% | -- |
| Female | 0.28 | -- |

| Characteristic | 1994 | 2005 |
|---|---|---|
| Race/Hispanic origin | | |
| White | 0.41% | 0.38% |
| Black /African American | 0.45 | 0.37 |
| Hispanic/Latino | 0.40 | 0.37 |
| Other | 0.08 | 0.13 |
| Age at release | | |
| 24 or younger | 0.37% | 0.30% |
| 25–29 | 0.40 | 0.32 |
| 30–34 | 0.40 | 0.30 |
| 35–39 | 0.35 | 0.30 |
| 40 or older | 0.35 | 0.38 |
| Most serious commitment offense | | |
| Violent | 0.11% | 0.36% |
| Property | 0.12 | 0.37 |
| Drug | 0.21 | 0.38 |
| Public order | 0.19 | 0.25 |

Source: Bureau of Justice Statistics, Recidivism of State Prisoners Released in 1994 and 2005 data collections.

-- Less than 0.005%.

## Appendix Table 2. Standard errors for table 2: Population-adjusted percent of prisoners arrested for a new crime within 3 years following release in 12 states in 1994 and 2005, by demographic characteristics and most serious commitment offense

| Characteristic | 1994 | 2005 |
|---|---|---|
| All released prisoners | 0.41% | 0.35% |
| Sex | | |
| Male | 0.43% | 0.38% |
| Female | 1.54 | 0.78 |
| Race/Hispanic origin | | |
| White | 0.72% | 0.60% |
| Black/African American | 0.56 | 0.49 |
| Hispanic/Latino | 1.05 | 0.92 |
| Other | 4.66 | 2.70 |
| Age at release | | |
| 24 or younger | 0.81% | 0.73% |
| 25–29 | 0.87 | 0.75 |
| 30–34 | 0.89 | 0.89 |
| 35–39 | 1.01 | 0.86 |
| 40 or older | 1.08 | 0.66 |
| Most serious commitment offense | | |

**Appendix Table 2. (Continued)**

| Characteristic | 1994 | 2005 |
|---|---|---|
| Violent | 0.69% | 0.68% |
| Property | 0.70 | 0.65 |
| Drug | 0.78 | 0.63 |
| Public order | 1.40 | 1.00 |

Source: Bureau of Justice Statistics, Recidivism of State Prisoners Released in 1994 and 2005 data collections.

**Appendix Table 3. Standard errors for table 3: First arrest charge of prisoners arrested for a new crime within 3 years following release in 11 states in 1994 and 2005**

| Most serious arrest charge | 1994 | 2005 |
|---|---|---|
| Violent | 0.47% | 0.35% |
| Property | 0.55 | 0.43 |
| Drug | 0.57 | 0.45 |
| Public order | 0.47 | 0.51 |
| Estimated number of prisoners with a post-release arrest | 1,053.17 | 978.74 |

Source: Bureau of Justice Statistics, Recidivism of State Prisoners Released in 1994 and 2005 data collections.

**Appendix Table 4. Standard errors for table 4: Population-adjusted percent of prisoners arrested for a violent crime within 3 years following release in 11 states in 1994 and 2005, by demographic characteristics and most serious commitment offense**

| Characteristic | 1994 | 2005 |
|---|---|---|
| All released prisoners | 0.39% | 0.38% |
| Sex | | |
| Male | 0.41% | 0.40% |
| Female | 0.96 | 0.93 |
| Race/Hispanic origin | | |
| White | 0.58% | 0.58% |
| Black/African American | 0.63 | 0.58 |
| Hispanic/Latino | 0.87 | 0.86 |
| Other | 3.07 | 5.17 |
| Age at release | | |
| 24 or younger | 0.93% | 0.91% |
| 25–29 | 0.85 | 0.86 |

| | | |
|---|---|---|
| 30–34 | 0.84 | 0.85 |
| 35–39 | 0.85 | 0.85 |
| 40 or older | 0.81 | 0.64 |
| Most serious commitment offense | | |
| Violent | 0.73% | 0.72% |
| Property | 0.67 | 0.72 |
| Drug | 0.71 | 0.67 |
| Public order | 1.20 | 0.94 |

Source: Bureau of Justice Statistics, Recidivism of State Prisoners Released in 1994 and 2005 data collections.

### Appendix Table 5. Standard errors for table 5: Characteristics of prisoners released in 30 states in 2005

| Characteristic | Percent |
|---|---|
| Sex | |
| Male | -- |
| Female | -- |
| Race/Hispanic origin | |
| White | 0.28% |
| Black/African American | 0.27 |
| Hispanic/Latino | 0.26 |
| Other | 0.09 |
| Age at release | |
| 24 or younger | 0.22% |
| 25–29 | 0.24 |
| 30–34 | 0.22 |
| 35–39 | 0.22 |
| 40 or older | 0.28 |
| Most serious commitment offense | |
| Violent | 0.26% |
| Property | 0.28 |
| Drug | 0.28 |
| Public order | 0.18 |
| Number of prior arrests per released prisoner | |
| 2 or fewer | 0.15% |
| 3–4 | 0.18 |
| 5–9 | 0.27 |
| 10 or more | 0.29 |
| Mean number | 0.06 |
| Median number | 0.05 |
| Number of prior convictions per released prisoner | |
| Mean number | 0.03 |

**Appendix Table 5. (Continued)**

| Characteristic | Percent |
|---|---|
| Median number | 0.03 |

**Appendix Table 6. Standard errors for table 6: Out-of-state arrests of prisoners released in 30 states in 2005 arrests**

| Out-of-state arrests | Percent |
|---|---|
| Prior to release | |
| 1 or more | 0.24% |
| 1–4 | 0.21 |
| 5–9 | 0.11 |
| 10 or more | 0.09 |
| Post-release 1 or more | 0.16% |
| 1–4 | 0.15 |
| 5–9 | 0.05 |
| 10 or more | 0.02 |

Source: Bureau of Justice Statistics, Recidivism of State Prisoners Released in 2005 data collection.

**Appendix Table 7. Standard errors for figure 2: Percent of prisoners arrested during the year who had not been arrested since release in30 states in 2005**

| Year after release | Annual failure rate |
|---|---|
| Year 1 | 0.29% |
| Year 2 | 0.33 |
| Year 3 | 0.34 |
| Year 4 | 0.34 |
| Year 5 | 0.34 |

Source: Bureau of Justice Statistics, Recidivism of State Prisoners Released in 2005 data collection.

**Appendix Table 8. Standard errors for table 7: Post-release arrests of prisoners released in 30 states in 2005**

| Post-release arrests | Percent |
|---|---|
| None | 0.23% |
| 1 | 0.22 |
| 2 | 0.21 |

| Post-release arrests | Percent |
|---|---|
| 3 | 0.19 |
| 4 | 0.17 |
| 5 | 0.16 |
| 6 or more | 0.24 |
| Estimated number of post-release arrests | 8,328.32 |
| Mean number per released prisoners | 0.02 |
| Median number per released prisoners | 0.02 |

Source: Bureau of Justice Statistics, Recidivism of State Prisoners Released in 2005 data collection.

### Appendix Table 9. Standard errors for table 8: Recidivism of prisoners released in 30 states in 2005, by most serious commitment offense and time from release to first arrest

| Most serious commitment offense | 6 months | Cumulative percent of released prisoners arrested within— 1 year | 2 years | 3 years | 4 years | 5 years |
|---|---|---|---|---|---|---|
| All released prisoners | 0.28% | 0.29% | 0.27% | 0.25% | 0.24% | 0.23% |
| Violent | 0.56% | 0.60% | 0.58% | 0.55% | 0.52% | 0.50% |
| Homicide | 0.04 | 0.05 | 0.06 | 0.06 | 0.06 | 0.06 |
| Murder | 0.05 | 0.06 | 0.08 | 0.08 | 0.08 | 0.08 |
| Nonnegligent manslaughter | 0.12 | 0.16 | 0.18 | 0.19 | 0.19 | 0.19 |
| Negligent manslaughter | 0.06 | 0.08 | 0.09 | 0.10 | 0.10 | 0.10 |
| Rape/sexual assault | 1.19 | 1.33 | 1.37 | 1.35 | 1.33 | 1.30 |
| Robbery | 1.02 | 1.07 | 1.02 | 0.96 | 0.92 | 0.85 |
| Assault | 1.04 | 1.09 | 1.03 | 0.96 | 0.90 | 0.84 |
| Other | 2.25 | 2.27 | 2.12 | 2.01 | 1.94 | 1.85 |
| Property | 0.56% | 0.55% | 0.49% | 0.45% | 0.41% | 0.39% |
| Burglary | 0.87 | 0.88 | 0.80 | 0.73 | 0.68 | 0.64 |
| Larceny/motor vehicle theft | 1.06 | 1.01 | 0.89 | 0.81 | 0.75 | 0.71 |
| Fraud/forgery | 1.13 | 1.15 | 1.07 | 0.98 | 0.93 | 0.87 |
| Other | 1.63 | 1.62 | 1.44 | 1.26 | 1.13 | 1.06 |
| Drug | 0.51% | 0.53% | 0.50% | 0.46% | 0.43% | 0.41% |
| Possession | 1.00 | 1.04 | 0.97 | 0.90 | 0.82 | 0.78 |
| Trafficking | 0.78 | 0.82 | 0.77 | 0.72 | 0.68 | 0.65 |
| Other | 0.93 | 0.97 | 0.88 | 0.80 | 0.74 | 0.68 |
| Public order | 0.74% | 0.77% | 0.74% | 0.70% | 0.67% | 0.64% |
| Weapons | 1.92 | 1.87 | 1.66 | 1.51 | 1.43 | 1.36 |

**Appendix Table 9. (Continued)**

| Most serious commitment offense | 6 months | Cumulative percent of released prisoners arrested within— 1 year | 2 years | 3 years | 4 years | 5 years |
|---|---|---|---|---|---|---|
| Driving under the influence | 1.07 | 1.24 | 1.38 | 1.41 | 1.39 | 1.36 |
| Other | 0.92 | 0.98 | 0.93 | 0.87 | 0.82 | 0.76 |

Source: Bureau of Justice Statistics, Recidivism of State Prisoners Released in 2005 data collection.

**Appendix Table 10. Standard errors for table 9: Recidivism of prisoners released in 30 states in 2005, by type of post-release arrest charge**

| *Post-release arrest charge* | *Percent of released prisoners arrested within 5 years of release* |
|---|---|
| *Any offense* | 0.23% |
| *Violent* | 0.27% |
| Homicide | 0.06 |
| Rape/sexual assault | 0.08 |
| Robbery | 0.15 |
| Assault | 0.25 |
| Other | 0.12 |
| *Property* | 0.29% |
| Burglary | 0.19 |
| Larceny/motor vehicle theft | 0.24 |
| Fraud/forgery | 0.20 |
| Other | 0.24 |
| *Drug* | 0.29% |
| Possession | 0.27 |
| Trafficking | 0.21 |
| Other | 0.25 |
| *Public order* | 0.27% |
| Weapons | 0.19 |
| Driving under the influence | 0.18 |
| Probation/parole violation | 0.26 |
| Other | 0.29 |

Source: Bureau of Justice Statistics, Recidivism of State Prisoners Released in 2005 data collection.

**Appendix Table 11. Standard errors for table 10: Recidivism of prisoners released in 30 states in 2005, by type of post-release arrest charge and most serious commitment offense**

| Most serious | | Percent of released prisoners arrested | | | |
|---|---|---|---|---|---|
| commitment offense | Any offense | Violent | Property | Drug | Public order |
| All released prisoners | 0.23% | 0.27% | 0.29% | 0.29% | 0.27% |
| Violent | 0.50 | 0.57 | 0.55 | 0.56 | 0.57 |
| Property | 0.39 | 0.50 | 0.56 | 0.56 | 0.51 |
| Drug | 0.41 | 0.47 | 0.51 | 0.53 | 0.50 |
| Public order | 0.64 | 0.71 | 0.73 | 0.73 | 0.72 |

Source: Bureau of Justice Statistics, Recidivism of State Prisoners Released in 2005 data collection.

**Appendix Table 12. Standard errors for table 11: Recidivism of prisoners released in 30 states in 2005, by prior arrest history, most serious commitment offense, and time from release to first arrest**

| Prior arrest | | Cumulative percent of released prisoners | | | | |
|---|---|---|---|---|---|---|
| serious | 6 months | 1 year | 2 years | 3 years | 4 years | 5 years |
| All released | 0.28% | 0.29% | 0.27% | 0.25% | 0.24% | 0.23% |
| 4 or fewer | 0.38% | 0.45% | 0.48% | 0.48% | 0.47% | 0.46% |
| Violent | 0.60 | 0.72 | 0.78 | 0.80 | 0.80 | 0.79 |
| Property | 0.83 | 0.98 | 1.05 | 1.03 | 1.00 | 0.98 |
| Drug | 0.72 | 0.82 | 0.90 | 0.90 | 0.88 | 0.86 |
| Public order | 1.17 | 1.30 | 1.33 | 1.30 | 1.27 | 1.24 |
| 5–9 | 0.48% | 0.52% | 0.50% | 0.47% | 0.44% | 0.42% |
| Violent | 1.02 | 1.09 | 1.07 | 1.01 | 0.96 | 0.93 |
| Property | 0.95 | 0.98 | 0.91 | 0.83 | 0.77 | 0.72 |
| Drug | 0.76 | 0.86 | 0.84 | 0.79 | 0.73 | 0.70 |
| Public order | 1.24 | 1.32 | 1.31 | 1.27 | 1.22 | 1.16 |
| 10 or more | 0.50% | 0.48% | 0.42% | 0.38% | 0.35% | 0.32% |
| Violent | 1.21 | 1.17 | 1.00 | 0.93 | 0.87 | 0.75 |
| Property | 0.85 | 0.80 | 0.66 | 0.59 | 0.53 | 0.50 |
| Drug | 0.90 | 0.87 | 0.77 | 0.69 | 0.63 | 0.58 |
| Public order | 1.27 | 1.28 | 1.14 | 1.02 | 0.96 | 0.92 |

Source: Bureau of Justice Statistics, Recidivism of State Prisoners Released in 2005 data collection.

**Appendix Table 13. Standard errors for table 12: Recidivism of prisoners released in 30 states in 2005, by sex of releasee, most serious commitment offense, and time from release to first arrest**

| Sex of releasee and most serious commitment offense | Cumulative percent of released prisoners arrested within— | | | | | |
|---|---|---|---|---|---|---|
| | 6 months | 1 year | 2 years | 3 years | 4 years | 5 years |
| All released prisoners | 0.28% | 0.29% | 0.27% | 0.25% | 0.24% | 0.23% |
| Male | 0.31% | 0.32% | 0.30% | 0.28% | 0.26% | 0.25% |
| Violent | 0.59 | 0.63 | 0.61 | 0.58 | 0.55 | 0.52 |
| Property | 0.63 | 0.62 | 0.55 | 0.50 | 0.46 | 0.44 |
| Drug | 0.57 | 0.59 | 0.55 | 0.51 | 0.48 | 0.45 |
| Public order | 0.80 | 0.83 | 0.80 | 0.75 | 0.71 | 0.68 |
| Female | 0.45% | 0.49% | 0.49% | 0.48% | 0.46% | 0.44% |
| Violent | 1.13 | 1.25 | 1.28 | 1.24 | 1.21 | 1.17 |
| Property | 0.79 | 0.85 | 0.84 | 0.80 | 0.76 | 0.73 |
| Drug | 0.77 | 0.83 | 0.83 | 0.80 | 0.78 | 0.75 |
| Public order | 1.20 | 1.36 | 1.42 | 1.39 | 1.34 | 1.30 |

Source: Bureau of Justice Statistics, Recidivism of State Prisoners Released in 2005 data collection.

**Appendix Table 14. Standard errors for table 13: Post-release arrests of prisoners released in 30 states in 2005, by sex of releasee**

| Post-release arrests | Male | Female |
|---|---|---|
| None | 0.25% | 0.44% |
| 1 | 0.25 | 0.38 |
| 2 | 0.23 | 0.36 |
| 3 | 0.21 | 0.31 |
| 4 | 0.19 | 0.28 |
| 5 | 0.17 | 0.27 |
| 6 or more | 0.26 | 0.38 |
| Estimated post-release arrests | 8,193.63 | 1,491.77 |
| Mean number | 0.02 | 0.03 |
| Median number | 0.02 | 0.03 |

Source: Bureau of Justice Statistics, Recidivism of State Prisoners Released in 2005 data collection.

**Appendix Table 15. Standard errors for table 14: Recidivism of prisoners released in 30 states in 2005, by age at release, most serious commitment offense, and time from release to first arrest**

| Age at release and most | | | Cumulative percent of released prisoners arrested within— | | | |
|---|---|---|---|---|---|---|
| serious commitment offense | 6 months | 1 year | 2 years | 3 years | 4 years | 5 years |
| All released prisoners | 0.28% | 0.29% | 0.27% | 0.25% | 0.24% | 0.23% |
| 24 or younger | 0.69% | 0.68% | 0.60% | 0.54% | 0.49% | 0.45% |
| Violent | 1.34 | 1.38 | 1.27 | 1.17 | 1.10 | 0.99 |
| Property | 1.23 | 1.17 | 1.00 | 0.89 | 0.80 | 0.74 |
| Drug | 1.21 | 1.23 | 1.05 | 0.93 | 0.82 | 0.77 |
| Public order | 2.15 | 2.04 | 1.80 | 1.65 | 1.48 | 1.27 |
| 25–29 | 0.67% | 0.68% | 0.62% | 0.55% | 0.51% | 0.48% |
| Violent | 1.31 | 1.37 | 1.29 | 1.16 | 1.07 | 0.99 |
| Property | 1.33 | 1.31 | 1.15 | 1.02 | 0.94 | 0.88 |
| Drug | 1.11 | 1.15 | 1.05 | 0.94 | 0.86 | 0.82 |
| Public order | 1.88 | 1.89 | 1.70 | 1.55 | 1.43 | 1.35 |
| 30–34 | 0.73% | 0.76% | 0.71% | 0.66% | 0.63% | 0.60% |
| Violent | 1.45 | 1.53 | 1.48 | 1.41 | 1.34 | 1.29 |
| Property | 1.44 | 1.42 | 1.27 | 1.15 | 1.05 | 1.00 |
| Drug | 1.23 | 1.31 | 1.24 | 1.17 | 1.10 | 1.05 |
| Public order | 1.95 | 1.97 | 1.86 | 1.74 | 1.68 | 1.58 |
| 35–39 | 0.75% | 0.77% | 0.71% | 0.65% | 0.61% | 0.57% |
| Violent | 1.53 | 1.61 | 1.44 | 1.35 | 1.28 | 1.24 |
| Property | 1.40 | 1.37 | 1.21 | 1.05 | 0.96 | 0.92 |
| Drug | 1.35 | 1.38 | 1.32 | 1.22 | 1.14 | 1.06 |
| Public order | 1.73 | 1.84 | 1.82 | 1.75 | 1.68 | 1.59 |
| 40 or older | 0.51% | 0.54% | 0.52% | 0.50% | 0.48% | 0.46% |
| Violent | 0.95 | 1.05 | 1.06 | 1.05 | 1.02 | 0.99 |
| Property | 1.02 | 1.04 | 0.96 | 0.90 | 0.85 | 0.81 |
| Drug | 0.95 | 1.01 | 0.95 | 0.89 | 0.85 | 0.81 |
| Public order | 1.09 | 1.18 | 1.26 | 1.22 | 1.18 | 1.16 |

Source: Bureau of Justice Statistics, Recidivism of State Prisoners Released in 2005 data collection.

**Appendix Table 16. Standard errors for table 15: Recidivism of prisoners released in 30 states in 2005, by race or Hispanic origin, most serious commitment offense, and time from release to first arrest**

| Race/Hispanic origin and most serious commitment offense | Cumulative percent of released prisoners arrested within— | | | | | |
|---|---|---|---|---|---|---|
| | 6 months | 1 year | 2 years | 3 years | 4 years | 5 years |
| All released prisoners | 0.28% | 0.29% | 0.27% | 0.25% | 0.24% | 0.23% |
| White | 0.42% | 0.44% | 0.42% | 0.39% | 0.37% | 0.35% |
| Violent | 0.85 | 0.93 | 0.92 | 0.89 | 0.86 | 0.83 |
| Property | 0.75 | 0.74 | 0.67 | 0.61 | 0.57 | 0.54 |
| Drug | 0.88 | 0.93 | 0.87 | 0.81 | 0.75 | 0.71 |
| Public order | 0.90 | 0.97 | 0.98 | 0.93 | 0.89 | 0.86 |
| Black/African American | 0.41% | 0.42% | 0.39% | 0.35% | 0.33% | 0.30% |
| Violent | 0.80 | 0.83 | 0.77 | 0.71 | 0.66 | 0.59 |
| Property | 0.89 | 0.88 | 0.78 | 0.71 | 0.63 | 0.60 |
| Drug | 0.67 | 0.69 | 0.63 | 0.57 | 0.53 | 0.49 |
| Public order | 1.20 | 1.24 | 1.16 | 1.09 | 1.02 | 0.94 |
| Hispanic/Latino | 0.91% | 0.93% | 0.87% | 0.81% | 0.78% | 0.75% |
| Violent | 1.69 | 1.78 | 1.73 | 1.64 | 1.58 | 1.51 |
| Property | 1.88 | 1.84 | 1.60 | 1.46 | 1.41 | 1.32 |
| Drug | 1.50 | 1.57 | 1.50 | 1.40 | 1.33 | 1.30 |
| Public order | 2.68 | 2.68 | 2.53 | 2.38 | 2.29 | 2.19 |
| Other | 1.77% | 1.97% | 1.85% | 1.71% | 1.62% | 1.57% |
| Violent | 2.76 | 3.41 | 3.50 | 3.37 | 3.33 | 3.21 |
| Property | 3.79 | 3.58 | 3.17 | 2.56 | 2.47 | 2.43 |
| Drug | 2.98 | 4.57 | 4.47 | 4.18 | 3.40 | 3.37 |
| Public order | 3.15 | 3.45 | 3.43 | 3.30 | 3.27 | 3.27 |

Source: Bureau of Justice Statistics, Recidivism of State Prisoners Released in 2005 data collection.

**Appendix Table 17. Standard errors for table 16: Recidivism of prisoners released in 29 states in 2005, by most serious commitment offense and time from release to first arrest that led to recidivating event**

| Recidivism measurement and most | | Cumulative percent of released prisoners who recidivated within— | | | | |
|---|---|---|---|---|---|---|
| serious commitment offense | 6 months | 1 year | 2 years | 3 years | 4 years | 5 years |
| Adjudication | 0.23% | 0.27% | 0.30% | 0.31% | 0.30% | 0.30% |
| Violent | 0.40 | 0.49 | 0.57 | 0.59 | 0.60 | 0.60 |
| Property | 0.46 | 0.54 | 0.57 | 0.57 | 0.56 | 0.55 |
| Drug | 0.42 | 0.50 | 0.54 | 0.55 | 0.54 | 0.53 |
| Public order | 0.58 | 0.68 | 0.76 | 0.78 | 0.78 | 0.77 |
| Conviction | 0.21% | 0.26% | 0.29% | 0.30% | 0.31% | 0.30% |
| Violent | 0.37 | 0.46 | 0.55 | 0.58 | 0.60 | 0.60 |
| Property | 0.43 | 0.52 | 0.56 | 0.57 | 0.57 | 0.56 |
| Drug | 0.39 | 0.47 | 0.53 | 0.55 | 0.55 | 0.54 |
| Public order | 0.55 | 0.67 | 0.75 | 0.78 | 0.78 | 0.78 |
| Incarceration | 0.19% | 0.24% | 0.28% | 0.29% | 0.30% | 0.30% |
| Violent | 0.35 | 0.43 | 0.51 | 0.55 | 0.58 | 0.59 |
| Property | 0.39 | 0.48 | 0.54 | 0.56 | 0.57 | 0.57 |
| Drug | 0.33 | 0.42 | 0.50 | 0.52 | 0.54 | 0.54 |
| Public order | 0.49 | 0.61 | 0.71 | 0.76 | 0.78 | 0.78 |
| Imprisonment | 0.15% | 0.20% | 0.24% | 0.26% | 0.27% | 0.28% |
| Violent | 0.27 | 0.34 | 0.43 | 0.47 | 0.50 | 0.53 |
| Property | 0.33 | 0.42 | 0.48 | 0.52 | 0.54 | 0.55 |
| Drug | 0.25 | 0.33 | 0.42 | 0.46 | 0.48 | 0.50 |
| Public order | 0.38 | 0.49 | 0.62 | 0.68 | 0.71 | 0.73 |
| Return to prison | 0.30% | 0.33% | 0.34% | 0.33% | 0.33% | 0.33% |
| Violent | 0.62 | 0.70 | 0.71 | 0.71 | 0.70 | 0.69 |
| Property | 0.61 | 0.65 | 0.64 | 0.62 | 0.61 | 0.60 |
| Drug | 0.52 | 0.60 | 0.62 | 0.62 | 0.61 | 0.61 |
| Public order | 0.80 | 0.91 | 0.93 | 0.91 | 0.90 | 0.89 |

Source: Bureau of Justice Statistics, Recidivism of State Prisoners Released in 2005 data collection.

## End Notes

* These estimates were based on prisoners released in the 11 states in both studies that included charge descriptions in their criminal history records.

[1] Link Plus Version 2.10 probabilistic record linkage software. Atlanta, GA: Centers for Disease Control and Prevention, 2006.

[2] Fellegi, I. P., & Sunter, A. B. (1969). A theory for record linkage. Journal of the American Statistical Association, 64, 1183–12.

# INDEX

## A



## B

## E



## F

## G



## H



## I



## J

## Q



## R



## S

## T